THE CONTEMPORARY SHAKESPEARE

Edited by A. L. Rowse

The Winter's Tale

Modern Text with Introduction

UNIVERSITY PRESS OF AMERICA

Copyright © 1985 by A. L. Rowse

University Press of America,® Inc.

4720 Boston Way
Lanham, MD 20706

3 Henrietta Street
London WC2E 8LU England

Distributed to the trade by The Scribner Book Companies

Library of Congress Cataloging in Publication Data

Shakespeare, William, 1564-1616.
  The winter's tale.

  (The Contemporary Shakespeare)
  I. Rowse, A. L. (Alfred Leslie), 1903-   .
II. Title. III. Series: Shakespeare, William, 1564-
1616. Plays (University Press of America : Pbk. ed.)
PR2839.A2R68 1985   822.3'3   85-22751
ISBN 0-8191-3924-6 (pbk.)

This play is also available as part of Volume IV in a seven volume
clothbound and slipcased set.

Book design by Leon Bolognese

WHY A CONTEMPORARY SHAKESPEARE?

The starting point of my project was when I learned both from television and in education, that Shakespeare is being increasingly dropped in schools and colleges because of the difficulty of the language. In some cases, I gather, they are given just a synopsis of the play, then the teacher or professor embroiders from his notes.

This is deplorable. We do not want Shakespeare progressively dropped because of superfluous difficulties that can be removed, skilfully, conservatively, keeping to every line of the text. Nor must we look at the question statically, for this state of affairs will worsen as time goes on and we get further away from the language of 400 years ago—difficult enough in all conscience now.

We must begin by ridding our mind of prejudice, i.e. we must not pre-judge the matter. A friend of mine on New York radio said that he was 'appalled' at the very idea; but when he heard my exposition of what was proposed he found it reasonable and convincing.

Just remember, I do not need it myself: *I live in the Elizabethan age*, Shakespeare's time, and have done for years, and am familiar with its language, and his. But even for me there are still difficulties—still more for modern people, whom I am out to help.

Who, precisely?

Not only students at school and in college, but all readers of Shakespeare. Not only those, but all viewers of the plays, in the theatre, on radio and television—actors too, who increasingly find pronunciation of the words difficult, particularly obsolete ones—and there are many, besides the difficulty of accentuation.

The difficulties are naturally far greater for non-English-speaking peoples. We must remember that he is our greatest asset, and that other peoples use him a great deal in learning our language. There are no Iron Curtains for him—though, during Mao's Cultural Revolution in China, he was prohibited. Now that the ban has been lifted, I learn that the Chinese in thousands flock to his plays.

Now, a good deal that was grammatical four hundred years ago is positively ungrammatical today. We might begin by removing what is no longer good grammar.

For example: plural subjects with a verb in the singular:

'*Is* Bushy, Green and the earl of Wiltshire dead?' Any objection to replacing 'is' correctly by 'are'? Certainly not. I notice that some modern editions already correct—

These high wild hills and rough uneven ways

Draw*s* out our miles and make*s* them wearisome

to 'draw' and 'make', quite sensibly. Then, why not go further and regularise this Elizabethan usage to modern, consistently throughout?

Similarly with archaic double negatives—'Nor shall you not think neither'—and double comparatives: 'this is more worser than before.' There are hundreds of instances of what is now just bad grammar to begin with.

There must be a few thousand instances of superfluous subjunctives to reduce to simplicity and sense. Today we use the subjunctive occasionally after 'if', when we say 'if it be'. But we mostly say today 'if it is'. Now Shakespeare has hundreds of subjunctives, not only after if, but after though, although, unless, lest, whether, until, till, etc.

I see no point whatever in retaining them. They only add superfluous trouble in learning English, when the great appeal of our language as a world-language is precisely that it has less grammar to learn than almost any. Russian is unbelievably complicated. Inflected languages—German is like Latin in this respect—are really rather backward; it has been a great recommendation that English has been more progressive in this respect in simplifying itself.

Now we can go further along this line: keep a few subjunctives, if you must, but reduce them to a minimum.

Let us come to the verb. It is a great recommendation to modern English that our verbs are comparatively simple to conjugate — unlike even French, for example. In the Elizabethan age there was a great deal more of it, and some of it inconsistent in modern usage. Take Shakespeare's,

'Where is thy husband now? Where be thy brothers?'
Nothing is lost by rendering this as we should today:

Where is your husband now? Where are your brothers?

And so on.

The second and third person singular—all those shouldsts and wouldsts, wilts and shalts, haths and doths, have become completely obsolete. Here a vast simplification may be effected—with no loss as far as I can see, and with advantages from several points of view.

For example, 'st' at the end of a word is rather diffi-cult to say, and more difficult even for us when it is succeeded by a word beginning with 'th'. Try saying, 'Why usurpedst thou this?' Foreigners have the greatest difficulty in pronouncing our 'th' anyway—many never succeed in getting it round their tongues. Many of these tongue-twisters even for us proliferate in Shakespeare, and I see no objection to getting rid of *superfluous* diffi-culties. Much easier for people to say, 'Why did you usurp this?'—the same number of syllables too.

This pre-supposes getting rid of almost all thous and thees and thines. I have no objection to keeping a few here and there, if needed for a rhyme—even then they are sometimes not necessary.

Some words in Shakespeare have changed their meaning into the exact opposite: we ought to remove that stumbling-block. When Hamlet says, 'By heaven, I'll make a ghost of him that *lets* me', he means *stops*; and we should replace it by stops, or holds me. Shakespeare regularly uses the word 'owe' where we should say own: the meaning has changed. Take a line like, 'Thou dost here usurp the name thou ow'st not': we should say, 'You do here usurp the name you own not', with the bonus of getting rid of two ugly 'sts'.

The word 'presently' in the Elizabethan age did not mean in a few minutes or so, but immediately—in-stantly has the same number of syllables. 'Prevent' then had its Latin meaning, to go before, or forestall. Shakespeare frequently uses the word 'still' for always or ever.

Let us take the case of many archaic forms of words, simple one-syllable words that can be replaced without the slightest difference to the scansion: 'sith' for since, 'wrack' for wreck, 'holp' for helped, 'writ' for wrote, 'brake' for broke, 'spake' for spoke, 'bare' for bore, etc.

These give no trouble, nor do a lot of other words that he uses: 'repeal' for recall, 'reproof' for disproof, 'decline' for incline. A few words do give more trouble. The linguistic scholar, C. T. Onions, notes that it is sometimes difficult to give the precise meaning Shakespeare attaches to the word 'conceit'; it usually means thought, or fancy, or concept. I do not know that it ever has our meaning; actually the word 'conceited' with him means ingenious or fantastic, as 'artificial' with Elizabethans meant artistic or ingenious.

There is a whole class of words that have completely gone out, of which moderns do not know the meaning. I find no harm in replacing the word 'coistrel' by rascal, which is what it means—actually it has much the same sound—or 'coil' by fuss; we find 'accite' for summon, 'indigest' for formless. Hamlet's word 'reechy', for the incestuous kisses of his mother and her brother-in-law, has gone out of use: the nearest word, I suppose, would be reeky, but filthy would be a suitable modern equivalent.

In many cases it is extraordinary how little one would need to change, how conservative one could be. Take Hamlet's famous soliloquy, 'To be or not to be.' I find only two words that moderns would not know the meaning of, and one of those we might guess:

> . . .When he himself might his *quietus* make
> With a bare bodkin? Who would *fardels* bear. . .

'Quietus' means put paid; Elizabethans wrote the Latin 'quietus est' at the bottom of a bill that was paid—when it was—to say that it was settled. So that you could replace 'quietus' by settlement, same number of syllables, though not the same accentuation; so I would prefer to use the word acquittance, which has both.

'Fardels' means burdens; I see no objection to rendering, 'Who would burdens bear'—same meaning, same number of syllables, same accent: quite simple. I expect all the ladies to know what a bodkin is: a long pin, or skewer.

Now let us take something really difficult—perhaps the most difficult passage to render in all Shakespeare. It is the virtuoso comic piece describing all the diseases that horseflesh is heir to, in *The Taming of the Shrew*. The horse is Petruchio's. President Reagan tells me that this is the one Shakespearean part that he played—and a very gallant one too. In Britain last year we saw a fine performance of his on horseback in Windsor Park alongside of Queen Elizabeth II—very familiar ground to William Shakespeare and Queen Elizabeth I, as we know from *The Merry Wives of Windsor*.

Here is a headache for us: Petruchio's horse (not President Reagan's steed) was 'possessed with the glanders, and like to mose in the chine; troubled with the lampass, infected with the fashions, full of windgalls, sped with spavins, rayed with the yellows, past cure of the fives, stark spoiled with the staggers, begnawn with the bots; swayed in the back, and shoulder-shotten; near-legged before, and with a half-cheeked bit, and a headstall of sheep's leather', etc.

What on earth are we to make of that? No doubt it raised a laugh with Elizabethans, much more familiarly acquainted with horseflesh than we are; but I doubt if Hollywood was able to produce a nag for Reagan that qualified in all these respects.

Now, even without his horsemanship, we can clear one fence at the outset: 'mose in the chine'. Pages of superfluous commentary have been devoted to that word 'mose'. There was no such Elizabethan word: it was simply a printer's misprint for 'mourn', meaning dripping or running; so it suggests a running sore. You would need to consult the *Oxford English Dictionary*, compiled on historical lines, for some of the words, others like 'glanders' country folk know and we can guess.

So I would suggest a rendering something like this: 'possessed with glanders, and with a running sore in the back; troubled in the gums, and infected in the glands; full of galls in the fetlocks and swollen in the joints; yellow with jaundice, past cure of the strangles; stark spoiled with the staggers, and gnawed by worms; swayed in the back and shoulder put out; near-legged before, and with a half-cheeked bit and headgear of sheep's leather', etc. That at least makes it intelligible.

Oddly enough, one encounters the greatest difficulty with the least important words and phrases, Elizabethan expletives and malapropisms, or salutations like God 'ild you, Godden, for God shield you, Good-even, and so on. 'God's wounds' was Elizabeth I's favourite swearword; it appears frequently enough in Victorian novels as 'Zounds'— I have never heard anyone use it. The word 'Marry!', as in the phrase 'Marry come up!' has similarly gone out, though a very old gentleman at All Souls, Sir Charles Oman, had heard the phrase in the back-streets of Oxford just after the 1914-18 war. 'Whoreson' is frequent on the lips of coarse fellows in Shakespeare: the equivalent in Britain today would be bloody, in America (I suppose) s.o.b.

Relative pronouns, who and which: today we use who for persons, which for things. In Elizabethan times the two were hardly distinguished and were interchangeable. Provokingly Shakespeare used the personal relative 'who' more frequently for impersonal objects, rivers, buildings, towns; and then he no less frequently uses 'which' for persons. This calls out to be regularised for the modern reader.

Other usages are more confusing. The word 'cousin'

was used far more widely by the Elizabethans for their kin: it included nephews, for instance. Thus it is confusing in the English History plays to find a whole lot of nephews—like Richard III's, whom he had made away with in the Tower of London—referred to and addressed as cousins. That needs regularisation today, in the interests of historical accuracy and to get the relationship clear. The word 'niece' was sometimes used of a grandchild—in fact this is the word Shakespeare used in his will for his little grand-daughter Elizabeth, his eventual heiress who ended up as Lady Barnard, leaving money to her poor relations the Hathaways at Stratford. The Latin word *neptis*, from which niece comes also meant grandchild—Shakespeare's grammar-school education at Stratford was in Latin, and this shows you that he often thought of a word in terms of its Latin derivation.

Malapropisms, misuse of words, sometimes mistaking of meanings, are frequent with uneducated people, and sometimes not only with those. Shakespeare transcribed them from lower-class life to raise a laugh, more frequently than any writer for the purpose. They are an endearing feature of the talk of Mistress Quickly, hostess of the Boar's Inn in East Cheapside, and we have no difficulty in making out what she means. But in case some of us do, and for the benefit of non-native English speakers, I propose the correct word in brackets afterwards: 'You have brought her into such a canaries [quandary]. . .and she's as fartuous [virtuous] a civil, modest wife. . .'

Abbreviations: Shakespeare's text is starred—and in my view, marred—by innumerable abbreviations, which not only look ugly on the page but are sometimes difficult to pronounce. It is not easy to pronounce 'is't', or 'in't', or 'on't', and some others: if we cannot get rid of them altogether they should be drastically reduced. Similarly with 'i'th'', 'o'th'', with which the later plays are liberally bespattered, for "in the" or "of the."

We also have a quite unnecessary spattering of apos-
trophes in practically all editions of the plays—''d' for
the past participle, e.g. 'gather'd'. Surely it is much
better to regularise the past participle 'ed', e.g. gathered;
and when the last syllable is, far less frequently, to be
pronounced, then accent it, gatherèd.

This leads into the technical question of scansion,
where a practising poet is necessary to get the accents
right, to help the reader, and still more the actor. Most
people will hardly notice that, very often, the frequent
ending of words in 'ion', like reputation, has to be pronounced with two syllables at the end. So I propose to accent this when necessary, e.g. reputatiòn. I have noticed
the word 'ocean' as tri-syllabic, so I accent it, to help,
oceàn. A number of words which to us are monosyllables
were pronounced as two: hour, fire, tired; I sometimes
accent or give them a dieresis, either hoùr or fïre. In New
England speech words like prayèr, thëre, are apt to be
pronounced as two syllables—closer to Elizabethan
usage (as with words like gotten) than is modern speech
in Britain.

What I notice in practically all editions of Shakespeare's
plays is that the editors cannot be relied on to put the accents in the right places. One play edited by a well
known Shakespearean editor had, I observed, a dozen accents placed over the wrong syllables. This is under-
standable, for these people don't write poetry and do not
know how to scan. William Shakespeare knew all about
scanning, and you need to be both familiar with Elizabethan usage and a practising traditional poet to be able
to follow him.

His earlier verse was fairly regular in scansion, mostly
iambic pentameter with a great deal of rhyme. As time
went on he loosened out, until there are numerous irreg-
ular lines—this leaves us much freer in the matter of
modernising. Our equivalents should be rhythmically as

close as possible, but a strait-jacket need be no part of the equipment. A good Shakespearean scholar tells us, 'there is no necessity for Shakespeare's lines to scan absolutely. He thought of his verse as spoken rather than written and of his rhythmic units in terms of the voice rather than the page.'

There is nothing exclusive or mandatory about my project. We can all read Shakespeare in any edition we like— in the rebarbative olde Englishe spelling of the First Folio, if we wish. Any number of conventional academic editions exist, all weighed down with a burden of notes, many of them superfluous. I propose to make most of them unnecessary—only one occasionally at the foot of very few pages. Let the text be freed of superfluous difficulties, remove obstacles to let it speak for itself, while adhering conservatively to every line.

We really do not need any more editions of the Plays on conventional lines—more than enough of those exist already. But *A Contemporary Shakespeare* on these lines—both revolutionary and conservative—should be a help to everybody all round the world—though especially for younger people, increasingly with time moving away from the language of 400 years ago.

INTRODUCTION

This lovely play, which hovers for a good deal on the edge of the sorrowful (like the music of Mozart)—is classed as a comedy, for all ends happily. It is usual, and convenient, to class these last plays from *Pericles* onwards as romances, full as they are of improbable romantic happenings. These appealed greatly to the sophisticated audience of the Blackfriars theatre—much smaller than the Globe, covered over for indoor performances, more stage scenery and music—as also to the Jacobean Court, which hardly cared for brutal realism.

A great deal in it is calculated for a Court audience, with laughs that would specially appeal to it. Autolycus, the thieving pedlar—hence his name from the classical robber on the mountain-side, who escaped detection by changing the look of things—says in one of his disguises: 'Whether it likes me or no, I am a courtier. See you not the air of the Court in these enfoldings? [garments]. Has not my gait in it the measure of the Court? [A lofty strut]. Receives not your nose Court odour from me? [i.e. highly scented]. Reflect I not on your baseness, Court contempt?' etc.

The taking over of Blackfriars, hitherto a private theatre, by Shakespeare's Company, now the King's men, provided a new challenge to which he responded with two master-

pieces, *The Winter's Tale* and *The Tempest.* The experienced master was capable of a flexible dramaturgy for all
tastes—as we know, and has been proved throughout the
centuries since—and Simon Forman saw the play at the
Globe in May 1611.[1] He gives a fairly full account of
it, but was mainly interested—as he would be—in the
doings of Autolycus and drew the moral, as he usually
did: 'Beware of trusting feigned beggars or fawning fellows.'

It was performed at Court on Gunpowder day, 5 Novem-
ber, that year; and was chosen along with five others of the
master's plays—far more than anyone else's—for the grand
entertainments to celebrate Princess Elizabeth's marriage
to the Elector Palatine in 1613 (from which the present
royal line in Britain descends). An appropriate choice,
with the romantic marriage of the young princess of Sicilia
to the young prince of Bohemia. (But Bohemia! in only a
few years the foolish Elector would accept the Bohemian
throne and thus start the Thirty Years' War, incurring a
lifetime of exile for him and his Winter Queen. A winter's
tale indeed!—we see nature imitating art once more.)

Shakespeare got the outline of his story from Robert
Greene's early novel, *Pandosto,* the republication of which
in 1607 drew his attention to it, in the way usual with
him. But he changed a great deal. He made much more
of the psychotic jealousy King Leontes suffers from over
his wife, Hermione's, friendliness for his former friend,
Polixenes. In the course of it he creates a marvellous
character in the vein of King Lear, who learns truth and
repentance from the sufferings he endures—and inflicts.
In fact, Leontes is a completely modern study in psychosis;
the way it operates is borne out by the findings of contemporary psychiatry. We might say that only shock-treatment—
the death of his son, the presumed death of his wife,

[1] v. my *Simon Forman: Sex and Society in Shakespeare's Age,*
306–07.

corroborating the sentence of the Delphic Oracle—brings him to his senses, faces him with the truth, brings healing with repentance. But already in the 18th century Dr. Johnson saw how psychologically veracious this was, however improbable the romantic circumstances of the tale for a winter's hearthside.

As usual it is Shakespeare's own creations that are best. He entirely re-creates Leontes and fills out his relations with his Queen, spirited to begin with, then struck down by the madness, and jealousy of her husband; entirely innocent and forgiving, she has much in common with Queen Catherine in *Henry VIII*. Paulina, her lady in waiting, is a fine character fully portrayed: utterly loyal to the injured Queen, fearless and outspoken, she is not afraid to stand up to the King and tell him what she thinks. A suggestion of comedy, for she is rather loquacious, relieves the tension with her. Still more with Autolycus, one of Shakespeare's most appealing creations; there is a charm upon him, as he charms his victims with his patter and his songs, his quick transformations of character and disguises. An enchanting virtuoso of the roads—there is a suggestion that he had known employment about the Court, until dismissed for some misdemeanour, we do not know what. And O, the beauty of his songs!

When daffodils begin to peer,
    With heigh! the doxy over the dale,
Why then comes in the sweet of the year,
    For the red blood reigns in the winter's pale.

(We can imagine William Shakespeare at home at Stratford writing that.) No wonder all the country folk were taken in by Autolycus—I am with Simon Forman in finding my attention fixed by him and the delicious country life surrounding him, the shepherds' shearing feast, the three-men songs, the country folk bearing their part and thinking that what is in print must be true. All so true to the life of the age.

Professor Sisson notices that the story of Leontes and Hermione portrays the romance of middle age. No one notices that it is William Shakespeare getting older, looking back:

> Looking on the lines
> Of my boy's face, I thought I did recoil
> Twenty-three years, and saw myself unbreeched
> In my green velvet coat, my dagger muzzled
> Lest it should bite its master and so prove,
> As ornaments oft do, too dangerous.

Polixenes has a boy too:

> He's all my exercise, my mirth, my matter . . .
> He makes a July's day short as December.

Each has an only son. Leontes' boy dies—and Shakespeare knew that grief: his only son, who was to have carried on the name, had died as a boy of eleven. There was no boy to gladden the household at Stratford, which saw more of the master now, his strenuous hard-working days over.

The theme of gentility is there, and much is made of it. William Shakespeare had taken out his coat-of-arms, *Non sans droict* (indeed!), in his father's name, so as to have been born a gentleman:

> As you are certainly a gentleman, thereto
> Clerk-like experienced—which no less adorns
> Our gentry than our parents' noble names.

Sir Thomas Smith tells us at the time that university men were *ipso facto* gentlemen from their clerk-like experience.[2] Then, with his inveterate sense of humour, the dramatist makes a lot of fun of the theme later. The Clown: 'You denied to fight with me this other day, because I was no gentleman born. See you these clothes? Say you see them not and think me still no gentleman born! You were best say these robes are not gentleman born.' And so it goes on.

William Shakespeare did not qualify as a gentleman through being an actor: the theatre was his livelihood, his way of making his money. He was much more proud of being a poet. Dr. Johnson saw that: 'it is impossible for any man to rid his mind of his profession.' The authorship of Shakespeare has supplied him with a metaphor:

How would he look, to see his work, so noble,
Vilely bound up!

All the same, the theatre is ever-present. Autolycus had, or invented, an acquaintance who had put on a show of the Prodigal Son. Perdita, as mistress of the shepherds' feast:

It seems I play as I have seen them do
In Whitsun pastorals.

Camillo will have Prince Florizel (this romantic name had actually appeared earlier in Warwickshire)—who had come to the feast disguised as a country swain—'royally appointed as if the scene you play were mine.' Paulina, completely justified, and meeting her Queen's lost daughter: 'the dignity of this act was worth the audience of kings and princes, for by such was it acted.'—And such

---

[2] q. in G. W. Prothero, *Select Statutes and Documents . . . of Elizabeth and James I*, 177.

was Shakespeare's audience. The King sums up towards
the end:

> and on this stage
> —Where we offenders now—appear soul-vexed.

Do we detect a personal note in the reflection?—

> Prosperity is the very bond of love,
> Whose fresh complexion and whose heart together
> Affliction alters.

We certainly have his regular wooing of the audience in
Time, the Chorus:

> Of this allow
> If ever you have spent time worse than now;
> If never, yet that Time himself does say
> He wishes earnestly you never may.

Contemporary social actualities are there with the
endearing marketings for the feast: 'Three pound of sugar,
five pound of currants; rice—what will this sister of mine
do with rice? . . . I must have saffron to colour the warden
pies; mace; dates?—nutmegs seven; a root or two of ginger;
four pounds of prunes, and as many of raisins of the sun.'
The shearers are all good singers—'but one Puritan among
them, and he sings psalms to hornpipes.'

One notices a certain casualness in the late verse of the
master, for all its occasional beauties (especially in the
description of flowers)—with so many lines ending in
and, but, for, that, as. Never mind: the text offers few
difficulties, and I have modernised the punctuation to
help the reader. No sacrosanctity attaches to Elizabethan
punctuation: it was often that of a compositor. And I have
supplied accents, as throughout this edition, to help both
reader and speaker of the verse with its scansion.

CHARACTERS

LEONTES, King of Sicilia
MAMILLIUS, his son, the young Prince
CAMILLO
ANTIGONUS
CLEOMENES   four lords of Sicilia
DION
POLIXENES, King of Bohemia
FLORIZEL, Prince of Bohemia
ARCHIDAMUS, a lord of Bohemia
OLD SHEPHERD, *supposed* father of Perdita
CLOWN, his son
AUTOLYCUS, a rogue
A MARINER
A GAOLER
HERMIONE, Queen to Leontes
PERDITA, daughter to Leontes and Hermione
PAULINA, wife to Antigonus
EMILIA, a lady attending on Hermione
MOPSA
DORCAS   shepherdesses
OTHER LORDS AND GENTLEMEN, LADIES, OFFICERS, AND
SERVANTS, SHEPHERDS, AND SHEPHERDESSES
TIME, as Chorus

Scene: Sicilia and Bohemia

Act I

SCENE I
Sicilia. Leontes' palace.

Enter Camillo and Archidamus.

ARCHIDAMUS If you shall chance, Camillo, to visit Bohemia on the like occasion whereon my services are now on foot, you shall see, as I have said, great difference betwixt our Bohemia and your Sicilia.

CAMILLO I think this coming summer the King of Sicilia means to pay Bohemia the visitation which he justly owes him.

ARCHIDAMUS Wherein our entertainment shall shame us, we will be justified in our loves; for indeed—

CAMILLO Beseech you—

ARCHIDAMUS Verily, I speak it in the freedom of my knowledge. We cannot with such magnificence—in so rare—I know not what to say. We will give you sleepy drinks, that your senses—unintelligent of our insufficiency—may, though they cannot praise us, as little accuse us.

CAMILLO You pay a great deal too dear for what is given freely.

ARCHIDAMUS Believe me, I speak as my understanding instructs me and as my honesty puts it to utterance.

CAMILLO Sicilia cannot show himself over-kind to Bohemia. They were trained together in their childhoods, and there rooted between them then such an affection which cannot choose but branch now. Since their more mature dignities and royal necessities made separation of their society, their encounters, though not personal, have been royally

attorneyed with interchange of gifts, letters, loving
embassies; that they have seemed to be together, though
absent; shook hands, as over a waste; and embraced, as
it were, from the ends of opposed winds. The heavens
continue their loves!

ARCHIDAMUS I think there is not in the world either
malice or matter to alter it. You have an unspeakable
comfort of your young prince Mamillius. It is a gentleman
of the greatest promise that ever came into my note.

CAMILLO I very well agree with you in the hopes of him.
It is a gallant child—one that indeed physics the subject,
makes old hearts fresh. They that went on crutches ere
he was born desire yet their life to see him a man.

ARCHIDAMUS Would they else be content to die?

CAMILLO Yes—if there were no other excuse why they
should desire to live.

ARCHIDAMUS If the king had no son, they would desire to
live on crutches till he had one.   *Exeunt.*

Scene II
The same.

Enter Leontes, Hermione, Mamillius, Polixenes,
Camillo, Lords.

POLIXENES
Nine changes of the watery star have been
The shepherd's note since we have left our throne
Without a burden. Time as long again
Would be filled up, my brother, with our thanks,
And yet we should, for perpetuity,
Go hence in debt. And therefore, like a cipher,
Yet standing in rich place, I multiply
With one 'We thank you' many thousands more
That go before it.

LEONTES   Stay your thanks a while
  And pay them when you part.
POLIXENES   Sir, that's to-morrow.
  I am questioned by my fears of what may chance
  Or breed upon our absence, that may blow
  No nipping winds at home to make us say,
  'This is put forth too truly.' Besides, I have stayed
  To tire your royalty.
LEONTES   We are tougher, brother,
  Than you can put us to it.
POLIXENES   No longer stay.
LEONTES
  One seven-night longer.
POLIXENES   Very true, to-morrow.
LEONTES
  We'll part the time between us then, and in that
  I'll no gainsaying.
POLIXENES   Press me not, beseech you, so.
  There is no tongue that moves, none in the world,
  So soon as yours could win me. So it should now
  Were there necessity in your request, although
  It were needful I denied it. My affairs
  Do even drag me homeward, which to hinder
  Were in your love a whip to me, my stay
  To you a charge and trouble. To save both,
  Farewell, our brother.
LEONTES   Tongue-tied our queen? Speak you.
HERMIONE
  I had thought, sir, to have held my peace until
  You had drawn oaths from him not to stay. You, sir,
  Charge him too coldly. Tell him you are sure
  All in Bohemia's well; this satisfaction
  The by-gone day proclaimed. Say this to him,
  He's beat from his best ward.
LEONTES   Well said, Hermione.

HERMIONE
  To tell he longs to see his son were strong.
  But let him say so then, and let him go;
  But let him swear so, and he shall not stay,
  We'll thwack him hence with distaffs.
  Yet of your royal presence I'll adventure
  The borrow of a week. When at Bohemia
  You take my lord, I'll give him my commission
  To leave him there a month behind the time
  Prefixed for his parting. Yet, good deed, Leontes,
  I love you not a tick of the clock behind
  Any lady she her lord. You'll stay?
POLIXENES   No, madam.
HERMIONE
  Nay, but you will?
POLIXENES   I may not, verily.
HERMIONE
  Verily?
  You put me off with feeble vows, but I,
  Though you would seek to unsphere the stars with
     oaths,
  Should yet say, 'Sir, no going.' Verily,
  You shall not go. A lady's 'Verily' is
  As potent as a lord's. Will you go yet?
  Force me to keep you as a prisoner,
  Not like a guest, so you shall pay your fees
  When you depart and save your thanks. How say you?
  My prisoner or my guest? By your dread 'Verily,'
  One of them you shall be.
POLIXENES   Your guest, then, madam.
  To be your prisoner should import offending,
  Which is for me less easy to commit
  Than you to punish.
HERMIONE   Not your gaoler, then,
  But your kind hostess. Come, I'll question you

Of my lord's tricks and yours when you were boys.
You were pretty lordings then?
POLIXENES   We were, fair queen,
Two lads that thought there was no more behind
But such a day to-morrow as to-day,
And to be boy eternal.
HERMIONE   Was not my lord
The verier wag of the two?
POLIXENES
We were as twinned lambs that did frisk in the sun,
And bleat the one at the other. What we changed
Was innocence for innocence; we knew not
The doctrine of ill-doing, nor dreamed
That any did. Had we pursued that life,
And our weak spirits never been higher reared
With stronger blood, we should have answered heaven
Boldly 'Not guilty,' the imposition cleared
Hereditary ours.
HERMIONE   By this we gather
You have tripped since.
POLIXENES   O my most sacred lady,
Temptations have since then been born to us, for
In those unfledged days was my wife a girl.
Your precious self had then not crossed the eyes
Of my young playfellow.
HERMIONE   Grace to goodness!
Of this make no conclusion, lest you say
Your queen and I are devils. Yet go on.
The offenses we have made you do we'll answer:
If you first sinned with us, and that with us
You did continue fault, and that you slipped not
With any but with us.
LEONTES   Is he won yet?
HERMIONE
He will stay, my lord.

LEONTES   At my request he would not.
  Hermione, my dearest, you never spoke
  To better purpose.
HERMIONE   Never?
LEONTES   Never but once.
HERMIONE
  What? Have I twice said well? When was it before?
  I pray tell me. Cram us with praise, and make us
  As fat as tame things. One good deed dying tongueless
  Slaughters a thousand waiting upon that.
  Our praises are our wages. You may ride us
  With one soft kiss a thousand furlongs ere
  With spur we heat an acre. But to the goal.
  My last good deed was to entreat his stay.
  What was my first? It has an elder sister,
  Or I mistake you. O, would her name were Grace!
  But once before I spoke to the purpose. When?
  Nay, let me have it; I long.
LEONTES   Why, that was when
  Three crabbèd months had soured themselves to death
  Ere I could make you open your white hand
  And clap yourself my love. Then did you utter
  'I am yours for ever.'
HERMIONE   It is grace indeed.
  Why, lo you now, I have spoken to the purpose twice;
  The one for ever earned a royal husband,
  The other for some while a friend.

Gives her hand to Polixenes, and they walk apart.

LEONTES [*aside*]   Too hot, too hot!
  To mingle friendship far is mingling bloods.
  I have tremor cordis[1] on me. My heart dances,
  But not for joy, not joy. This entertainment

---

[1]Palpitation of heart.

May a free face put on, derive a liberty
From heartiness, from bounty, fertile bosom,
And well become the agent. It may, I grant.
But to be paddling palms and pinching fingers,
As now they are, and making practiced smiles
As in a looking-glass, and then to sigh, as at
The death of the deer—O, that is entertainment
My bosom likes not, nor my brows. Mamillius,
Are you my boy?

MAMILLIUS   Ay, my good lord.

LEONTES In faith!
Why, that's my brave boy. What, smudged your nose?
They say it is a copy out of mine. Come, captain,
We must be neat—not neat but cleanly, captain.
And yet the steer, the heifer, and the calf
Are all called neat.—Still virginalling
Upon his palm?—How now, you wanton calf?
Are you my calf?

MAMILLIUS   Yes, if you will, my lord.

LEONTES
You want a rough head and the horns I have,
To be full like me; yet they say we are
Almost as like as eggs. Women say so,
That will say anything. But were they false
As over-dyed blacks, as wind, as waters, false
As dice are to be wished by one that fixes
No bourn between his and mine, yet were it true
To say this boy were like me. Come, sir page,
Look on me with your sky-blue eye. Sweet villain!
Most dearest! my treasure! Can your dam?—may it be?—
Affection, your intention stabs the center!
You do make possible things not so held,
Communicate with dreams—how can this be?
With what is unreal you coactive art,
And fellow nothing. Then it is very credent
You may co-join with something; and you do,

And that beyond commission, and I find it,
And that to the infection of my brains
And hardening of my brows.

POLIXENES   What means Sicilia?

HERMIONE

He something seems unsettled.

POLIXENES   How, my lord?
What cheer? How is it with you, best brother?

HERMIONE   You look
As if you held a brow of much distraction.
Are you moved, my lord?

LEONTES   No, in good earnest.
How sometimes nature will betray its folly,
Its tenderness, and make itself a pastime
To harder bosoms! Looking on the lines
Of my boy's face, I thought I did recoil
Twenty-three years, and saw myself unbreeched,
In my green velvet coat, my dagger muzzled
Lest it should bite its master and so prove,
As ornaments oft do, too dangerous.
How like, I thought, I then was to this kernel,
This squash, this gentleman. My honest friend,
Will you take eggs for money?

MAMILLIUS   No, my lord, I'll fight.

LEONTES

You will? Why, happy man be his lot! My brother,
Are you so fond of your young prince as we
Do seem to be of ours?

POLIXENES   If at home, sir,
He's all my exercise, my mirth, my matter,
Now my sworn friend and then my enemy,
My parasite, my soldier, statesman, all.
He makes a July's day short as December,
And with his varying childness cures in me
Thoughts that would thick my blood.

LEONTES   So stands this squire
  Officed with me. We two will walk, my lord,
  And leave you to your graver steps. Hermione,
  How you love us, show in our brother's welcome.
  Let what is dear in Sicily be cheap.
  Next to yourself and my young rover, he is
  Heir apparent to my heart.
HERMIONE   If you would seek us,
  We are yours in the garden. Shall we attend you there?
LEONTES
  To your own bents dispose you. You'll be found,
  Be you beneath the sky. [*aside*] I am angling now,
  Though you perceive me not how I give line.
  Go to, go to!
  How she holds up the beak, the bill to him,
  And arms her with the boldness of a wife
  To her allowing husband!
          Exeunt Polixenes, Hermione, and Attendants.
          Gone already!
  Inch-thick, knee-deep, o'er head and ears a forked one!
  Go play, boy, play. Your mother plays, and I
  Play too, but so disgraced a part, whose issue
  Will hiss me to my grave. Contempt and clamor
  Will be my knell. Go play, boy, play. There have been,
  Or I am much deceived, cuckolds ere now;
  And many a man there is, even at this present,
  Now while I speak this, holds his wife by the arm,
  That little thinks she has been sluiced in his absence
  And his pond fished by his next neighbor, by
  Sir Smile, his neighbor. Nay, there's comfort in it
  While other men have gates and those gates opened,
  As mine, against their will. Should all despair
  That have revolted wives, the tenth of mankind
  Would hang themselves. Physic for it there's none.
  It is a bawdy planet, that will strike
  Where 'tis predominant; it is powerful, think it,

From east, west, north, and south. Be it concluded,
No barricado for a belly. Know it,
It will let in and out the enemy
With bag and baggage. Many thousand of us
Have the disease and feel it not. How now, boy?

MAMILLIUS
I am like you, they say.

LEONTES   Why, that's some comfort.
What, Camillo there?

CAMILLO
Ay, my good lord.

LEONTES
Go play, Mamillius. You are an honest man.

Exit Mamillius.

Camillo, this great sir will yet stay longer.

CAMILLO
You had much ado to make his anchor hold;
When you cast out, it still came home.

LEONTES   Did you note it?

CAMILLO
He would not stay at your petitions, made
His business more material

LEONTES   Did you perceive it?

[*Aside.*]

They're here with me already, whispering, rounding
'Sicilia is a so-forth.' It is far gone,
When I shall taste it last. How came it, Camillo,
That he did stay?

CAMILLO   At the good queen's entreaty.

LEONTES
At the queen's be it. 'Good' should be pertinent;
But so it is, it is not. Was this taken
By any understanding pate but yours?
For your conceit is soaking, will draw in

More than the common blocks. Not noted, is it,
But of the finer natures, by several
Of head-piece extraordinary? Lower messes
Perchance are to this business purblind? Say.

CAMILLO
Business, my lord? I think most understand
Bohemia stays here longer.

LEONTES   Ha?

CAMILLO   Stays here longer.

LEONTES
Ay, but why?

CAMILLO
To satisfy your highness and the entreaties
Of our most gracious mistress.

LEONTES   Satisfy
The entreaties of your mistress? Satisfy;
Let that suffice. I have trusted you, Camillo,
With all the nearest things to my heart, as well
My chamber-councils, wherein, priest-like, you
Have cleansed my bosom, I from you departed
Your penitent reformed. But we have been
Deceived in your integrity, deceived
In that which seems so.

CAMILLO   Be it forbidden, my lord!

LEONTES
To bide upon it, you are not honest; or,
If you incline that way, you are a coward,
Which hamstrings honesty behind, restraining
From course required. Or else you must be counted
A servant grafted in my serious trust
And therein negligent. Or else a fool
That see a game played home, the rich stake drawn,
And take it all for jest.

CAMILLO   My gracious lord,
I may be negligent, foolish, and fearful.
In every one of these no man is free,

But that his negligence, his folly, fear,
Among the infinite doings of the world,
Sometimes puts forth. In your affairs, my lord,
If ever I were willful-negligent,
It was my folly; if industriously
I played the fool, it was my negligence,
Not weighing well the end. If ever fearful
To do a thing where I the issue doubted,
Whereof the execution did cry out
Against the non-performance, it was a fear
Which oft infects the wisest. These, my lord,
Are such allowed infirmities that honesty
Is never free of. But, beseech your grace,
Be plainer with me; let me know my trespass
By its own visage. If I deny it,
It is none of mine.

LEONTES   Have not you seen, Camillo—
But that's past doubt, you have, or your eye-glass
Is thicker than a cuckold's horn—or heard—
For to a vision so apparent rumor
Cannot be mute—or thought—for cogitation
Resides not in that man that does not think—
My wife is slippery? If you will confess,
Or else be impudently negative,
To have nor eyes nor ears nor thought, then say
My wife is a hobby-horse, deserves a name
As rank as any flax-wench that gives way
Before her troth-plight. Say it and justify it.

CAMILLO
I would not be a stander-by to hear
My sovereign mistress clouded so, without
My present vengeance taken. Bless my heart,
You never spoke what did become you less
Than this, which to reiterate were sin
As deep as that, though true.

LEONTES   Is whispering nothing?
　Is leaning cheek to cheek? Is meeting noses?
　Kissing with inside lip? stopping the career
　Of laughter with a sigh?—a note infallible
　Of breaking honesty!—horsing foot on foot?
　Skulking in corners? wishing clocks more swift?
　Hours, minutes? noon, midnight? and all eyes
　Blind with cataract but theirs, theirs only,
　That would unseen be wicked? Is this nothing?
　Why, then the world and all that's in it is nothing,
　The covering sky is nothing, Bohemia nothing,
　My wife is nothing, and nothing have these nothings,
　If this is nothing.
CAMILLO   Good my lord, be cured
　Of this diseased opinion, and betimes,
　For it is most dangerous.
LEONTES   Say it be, it is true.
CAMILLO
　No, no, my lord.
LEONTES   It is. You lie, you lie.
　I say you lie, Camillo, and I hate you,
　Pronounce you a gross lout, a mindless slave,
　Or else a hovering temporizer, that
　Can with your eyes at once see good and evil,
　Inclining to them both. Were my wife's liver
　Infected as her life, she would not live
　The running of one glass.
CAMILLO   Who does infect her?
LEONTES
　Why, he that wears her like her medal, hanging
　About his neck—Bohemia. Who, if I
　Had servants true about me that bore eyes
　To see alike my honor as their profits,　　　　　·
　Their own particular thrifts, they would do that
　Which should undo more doing. Ay, and you,
　His cupbearer—whom I from meaner form

Have benched and reared to worship, who may see
Plainly as heaven sees earth and earth sees heaven,
How I am gallèd—might bespice a cup
To give my enemy a lasting wink,
Which draught to me were cordial.

CAMILLO   Sir, my lord,
I could do this and that with no rash potion,
But with a lingering dram that should not work
Maliciously like poison. But I cannot
Believe this crack to be in my dread mistress,
So sovereignly being honorable.
I have loved you—

LEONTES   Make that your question, and go rot!
Do you think I am so muddy, so unsettled,
To appoint myself in this vexation, sully
The purity and whiteness of my sheets—
Which to preserve is sleep, which being spotted
Is goads, thorns, nettles, tails of wasps—
Give scandal to the blood of the prince my son,
Who I do think is mine and love as mine,
Without ripe moving to it? Would I do this?
Could man so flinch?

CAMILLO   I must believe you, sir.
I do, and will fetch off Bohemia for it.
Provided that, when he's removed, your highness
Will take again your queen as yours at first—
Even for your son's sake, and thereby for sealing
The injury of tongues in Courts and kingdoms
Known and allied to yours.

LEONTES   You do advise me
Even so as I my own course have set down.
I'll give no blemish to her honor, none.

CAMILLO   My lord,
Go then, and with a countenance as clear
As friendship wears at feasts, keep with Bohemia
And with your queen. I am his cupbearer.

If from me he has wholesome beverage,
Account me not your servant.
LEONTES   This is all.
Do it, and you have the one half of my heart;
Do it not, you split your own.
CAMILLO   I'll do it, my lord.
LEONTES
I will seem friendly, as you have advised me.   *Exit.*
CAMILLO
O miserable lady! But for me,
What case stand I in? I must be the poisoner
Of good Polixenes; and my ground to do it
Is the obedience to a master, one
Who in rebellion with himself will have
All that are his so too. To do this deed,
Promotion follows. If I could find example
Of thousands that had struck anointed kings
And flourished after, I'd not do it; but since
Nor brass nor stone nor parchment bears not one,
Let villainy itself forswear it. I must
Forsake the court. To do it, or no, is certain
To me a break-neck. Happy star reign now!
Here comes Bohemia.

Enter Polixenes.

POLIXENES   This is strange. I think
My favor here begins to warp. Not speak?
Good day, Camillo.
CAMILLO   Hail, most royal sir!
POLIXENES
What is the news in the Court?
CAMILLO   None rare, my lord.
POLIXENES
The king has on him such a countenance
As he had lost some province and a region

Loved as he loves himself. Even now I met him
With customary compliment; when he,
Wafting his eyes to the contrary, letting fall
A lip of much contempt, speeds from me, and
So leaves me to consider what is breeding
That changes thus his manners.

CAMILLO
I dare not know, my lord.

POLIXENES
How dare not? do not? Do you know and dare not
Be intelligent to me? It is thereabouts,
For, to yourself, what you do know, you must,
And cannot say you dare not. Good Camillo,
Your changed complexions are to me a mirror
Which shows me mine changed too; for I must be
A party in this alteration, finding
Myself thus altered with it.

CAMILLO   There is a sickness
Which puts some of us in distemper, but
I cannot name the disease, and it is caught
Of you that yet are well.

POLIXENES   How caught of me?
Make me not sighted like the basilisk.[2]
I have looked on thousands who have sped the better
By my regard, but killed none so. Camillo,
As you are certainly a gentleman, thereto
Clerk-like experienced—which no less adorns
Our gentry than our parents' noble names,
In whose succession we are gentle—I beseech you,
If you know aught which does behove my knowledge
Thereof to be informed, imprison it not
In ignorant concealment.

CAMILLO   I may not answer.

---

[2]Fabled creature whose look killed.

POLIXENES
A sickness caught of me, and yet I well?
I must be answered. Do you hear, Camillo?
I conjure you by all the parts of man
Which honor does acknowledge, whereof the least
Is not this suit of mine, that you declare
What incidence you do guess of harm
Is creeping toward me; how far off, how near;
Which way to be prevented, if to be;
If not, how best to bear it.
CAMILLO   Sir, I will tell you,
Since I am charged in honor and by him
That I think honorable. Therefore mark my counsel,
Which must be even as swiftly followed as
I mean to utter it, or both yourself and I
Cry 'Lost,' and so good night!
POLIXENES   On, good Camillo.
CAMILLO
I am appointed him to murder you.
POLIXENES
By whom, Camillo?
CAMILLO   By the king.
POLIXENES   For what?
CAMILLO
He thinks, nay, with all confidence he swears,
As he had seen it or been an instrument
To vice you to it, that you have touched his queen
Forbiddenly.
POLIXENES O, then my best blood turn
To an infected jelly and my name
Be yoked with his that did betray the Best!
Turn then my freshest reputation to
A savor that may strike the dullest nostril
Where I arrive, and my approach be shunned,
Nay, hated too, worse than the worst infection
That ever was heard or read!

CAMILLO   Swear his thought over
    By each particular star in heaven and
    By all their influences, you may as well
    Forbid the sea then to obey the moon
    As either by oath remove or counsel shake
    The fabric of his folly, whose foundation
    Is piled upon his faith and will continue
    The standing of his body.
POLIXENES   How should this grow?
CAMILLO
    I know not. But I am sure it is safer to
    Avoid what's grown than question how 'tis born.
    If therefore you dare trust my honesty,
    That lies enclosèd in this trunk which you
    Shall bear along impawned, away to-night!
    Your followers I will whisper to the business,
    And will by twos and threes at several posterns
    Clear them of the city. For myself, I'll put
    My fortunes to your service, which are here
    By this discovery lost. Be not uncertain,
    For, by the honor of my parents, I
    Have uttered truth, which if you seek to prove,
    I dare not stand by; nor shall you be safer
    Than one condemnèd by the king's own mouth,
    Thereon his execution sworn.
POLIXENES   I do believe you;
    I saw his heart in his face. Give me your hand.
    Be pilot to me and your places shall
    Still neighbor mine. My ships are ready and
    My people did expect my hence departure
    Two days ago. This jealousy
    Is for a precious creature. As she's rare,
    Must it be great; as his person is mighty,
    Must it be violent; and as he does conceive
    He is dishonored by a man who ever
    Professed love to him, his revenges must

In that be made more bitter. Fear overshades me.
Good expedition be my friend, and comfort
The gracious queen, part of his theme but nothing
Of his ill-taken suspicion! Come, Camillo.
I will respect you as a father if
You bear my life off hence. Let us away.

CAMILLO
It is in my authority to command
The keys of all the posterns. Please your highness
To take the urgent hour. Come, sir, away.   *Exeunt.*

Act II

SCENE I
The same.

Enter Hermione, Mamillius, and Ladies.

HERMIONE
   Take the boy to you. He so troubles me,
   It is past enduring.
LADY   Come, my gracious lord,
   Shall I be your playfellow?
MAMILLIUS   No, I'll none of you.
LADY
   Why, my sweet lord?
MAMILLIUS
   You'll kiss me hard and speak to me as if
   I were a baby still. I love you better.
SECOND LADY
   And why so, my lord?
MAMILLIUS   Not quite because
   Your brows are blacker. Yet black brows, they say,
   Become some women best, if there is not
   Too much hair there, but in a semicircle,
   Or a half-moon made with a pen.
SECOND LADY   Who taught you this?
MAMILLIUS
   I learned it out of women's faces. Pray now,
   What color are your eyebrows?
LADY   Blue, my lord.

MAMILLIUS

Nay, that's a mock. I have seen a lady's nose
That has been blue, but not her eyebrows.

LADY   Hark you.

The queen your mother rounds apace. We shall
Present our services to a fine new prince
One of these days, and then you'd wanton with us,
If we would have you.

SECOND LADY   She is spread of late

Into a goodly bulk. Good time encounter her!

HERMIONE

What wisdom stirs among you? Come, sir, now
I am for you again. Pray you sit by us
And tell us a tale.

MAMILLIUS   Merry or sad shall it be?

HERMIONE

As merry as you will.

MAMILLIUS

A sad tale is best for winter. I have one
Of sprites and goblins.

HERMIONE   Let's have that, good sir.

Come on, sit down. Come on, and do your best
To fright me with your sprites; you're powerful at it.

MAMILLIUS

There was a man—

HERMIONE   Nay, come sit down; then on.

MAMILLIUS

Dwelt by a churchyard. I will tell it softly;
Yon crickets shall not hear it.

HERMIONE   Come on, then,

And give it me in my ear.

Enter Leontes, Antigonus, Lords and guards.

LEONTES

Was he met there? his train? Camillo with him?

LORD

Behind the tuft of pines I met them. Never
Saw I men scour so on their way. I eyed them
Even to their ships.

LEONTES   How blest am I
In my just judgment, in my true opinion!
Alas, for lesser knowledge! how accursed
In being so blest! There may be in the cup
A spider steeped, and one may drink, depart,
And yet partake no venom, for his knowledge
Is not infected. But if one present
The abhorred ingredient to his eye, makes known
How he has drunk, he cracks his gorge, his sides,
With violent vomits. I have drunk, and seen the spider.
Camillo was his help in this, his pander.
There is a plot against my life, my crown.
All's true that is mistrusted. That false villain
Whom I employed was pre-employed by him.
He has discovered my design, and I
Remain a racked thing—yea, a very trick
For them to play at will. How came the posterns
So easily open?

LORD   By his great authority,
Which often has no less prevailed than so
On your command.

LEONTES   I know it too well.
Give me the boy. I am glad you did not nurse him.
Though he does bear some signs of me, yet you
Have too much blood in him.

HERMIONE   What is this? sport?

LEONTES

Bear the boy hence. He shall not come about her.
Away with him! and let her sport herself

With that she's big with, for 'tis Polixenes
Has made you swell thus.

HERMIONE   But I'd say he had not,
And I'll be sworn you would believe my saying,
However you lean to the nayward.

LEONTES   You, my lords,
Look on her, mark her well. Be but about
To say 'She is a goodly lady,' and
The justice of your hearts will thereto add
''Tis pity she's not honest, honorable.'
Praise her but for this her without-door form—
Which on my faith deserves high speech—and straight
The shrug, the hum or ha, these petty brands
That calumny does use—O, I am out,
That mercy does, for calumny will sear
Virtue itself—these shrugs, these hums and ha's,
When you have said she's goodly, come between
Ere you can say she's honest. But be it known,
From him that has most cause to grieve it should be,
She's an adulteress.

HERMIONE   Should a villain say so,
The most replenished villain in the world,
He were as much more villain. You, my lord,
Do but mistake.

LEONTES   You have mistaken, my lady,
Polixenes for Leontes. O you thing!
Which I'll not call a creature of your place,
Lest barbarism, making me the precedent,
Should a like language use to all degrees
And mannerly distinguishment leave out
Between the prince and beggar. I have said
She's an adulteress; I have said with whom.
More, she's a traitor and Camillo is
A confederate with her, and one that knows
What she should shame to know herself
But with her most vile principal, that she's

A bed-swerver, even as bad as those
That vulgars give boldest titles—ay, and privy
To this their late escape.
HERMIONE   No, by my life,
Privy to none of this. How will this grieve you,
When you shall come to clearer knowledge, that
You thus have published me! Gentle my lord,
You scarce can right me thoroughly then to say
You did mistake.
LEONTES   No. If I mistake
In those foundations which I build upon,
The center is not big enough to bear
A schoolboy's top. Away with her to prison!
He who shall speak for her is afar off guilty
But that he speaks.
HERMIONE   There's some ill planet reigns.
I must be patient till the heavens look
With an aspect more favorable. Good my lords,
I am not prone to weeping, as our sex
Commonly are; the want of which vain dew
Perchance shall dry your pities. But I have
That honorable grief lodged here which burns
Worse than tears drown. Beseech you all, my lords,
With thoughts so qualified as your charities
Shall best instruct you, measure me; and so
The king's will be performed.
LEONTES   Shall I be heard?
HERMIONE
Who is it that goes with me? Beseech your highness,
My women may be with me, for you see
My plight requires it. Do not weep, good fools;
There is no cause. When you shall know your mistress
Has deserved prison, then abound in tears
As I come out. This action I now go on
Is for my better grace. Adieu, my lord.

I never wished to see you sorry; now
I trust I shall. My women, come; you have leave.

LEONTES
Go, do our bidding. Hence!

Exit Queen, guarded, with Ladies.

LORD
Beseech your highness, call the queen again.

ANTIGONUS
Be certain what you do, sir, lest your justice
Prove violence, in which three great ones suffer,
Yourself, your queen, your son.

LORD   For her, my lord,
I dare my life lay down and will do it, sir,
Please you to accept it, that the queen is spotless
In the eyes of heaven and to you—I mean,
In this which you accuse her.

ANTIGONUS   If it proves
She's otherwise, I'll keep my stables where
I lodge my wife. I'll go in couples with her,
Than when I feel and see her no farther trust her;
For every inch of woman in the world,
Ay, every dram of woman's flesh is false,
If she is.

LEONTES Hold your peaces.

LORD   Good my lord—

ANTIGONUS
It is for you we speak, not for ourselves.
You are abused and by some putter-on
That will be damned for it. Would I knew the villain,
I would make hell for him. Be she honor-flawed,
I have three daughters—the eldest is eleven,
The second and the third, nine and some five—
If this proves true, they'll pay for it. By my honor,
I'll geld them all; fourteen they shall not see
To bring false generations. They are co-heirs,

And I had rather geld myself than they
Should not produce fair issue.
LEONTES   Cease; no more.
You smell this business with a sense as cold
As is a dead man's nose. But I do see it and feel it,
As you feel doing thus [*pinches Antigonus*], and see
    with it
The instruments that feel.
ANTIGONUS   If it is so,
We need no grave to bury honesty.
There's not a grain of it the face to sweeten
Of the whole dungy earth.
LEONTES   What? Lack I credit?
LORD
I had rather you did lack than I, my lord,
Upon this ground; and more it would content me
To have her honor true than your suspicion,
Be blamed for it how you might.
LEONTES   Why, what need we
Commune with you of this, but rather follow
Our forceful instigation? Our prerogative
Calls not your counsels, but our natural goodness
Imparts this, which if you—or stupified
Or seeming so in skill—cannot or will not
Relish a truth like us, inform yourselves
We need no more of your advice. The matter,
The loss, the gain, the ordering of it, is all
Properly ours.
ANTIGONUS And I wish, my liege,
You had only in your silent judgment tried it,
Without more overture.
LEONTES   How could that be?
Either you are most ignorant by age
Or you were born a fool. Camillo's flight,
Added to their familiarity—
Which was as gross as ever touched conjecture,

That lacked sight only, nought for approbation
But only seeing, all other circumstances
Made up to the deed—does push on this proceeding.
Yet, for a greater confirmation—
For in an act of this importance it were
Most piteous to be wild—I have dispatched in post
To sacred Delphos, to Apollo's temple,
Cleomenes and Dion, whom you know
Of stuffed sufficiency. Now from the oracle
They will bring all, whose spiritual counsel had,
Shall stop or spur me. Have I done well?

LORD
Well done, my lord.

LEONTES
Though I am satisfied and need no more
Than what I know, yet shall the oracle
Give rest to the minds of others, such as he
Whose ignorant credulity will not
Come up to the truth. So have we thought it good
From our free person she should be confined,
Lest the treachery of the two fled hence
Be left her to perform. Come, follow us.
We are to speak in public, for this business
Will raise us all.

ANTIGONUS [*aside*] To laughter, as I take it,
If the good truth were known.   *Exeunt.*

SCENE II
A prison.

Enter Paulina, a Gentleman and Attendants.

PAULINA
The keeper of the prison, call to him;
Let him have knowledge who I am.   *Exit Gentleman.*

                            Good lady,
No Court in Europe is too good for you.
What do you then in prison?

                Enter Gentleman with the Gaoler.

                            Now, good sir,
You know me, do you not?
GAOLER   For a worthy lady
And one whom much I honor.
PAULINA   Pray you then,
Conduct me to the queen.
GAOLER   I may not, madam.
To the contrary I have express commandment.
PAULINA
Here's ado,
To lock up honesty and honor from
The access of gentle visitors. Is it lawful, pray you,
To see her women? any of them? Emilia?
GAOLER
So please you, madam,
To put apart these your attendants, I
Shall bring Emilia forth.
PAULINA   I pray now, call her.
Withdraw yourselves.
                        Exeunt Gentleman and Attendants.
GAOLER   And, madam,
I must be present at your conference.
PAULINA
Well, be it so, pray.   *Exit Gaoler.*
Here's such ado to make no stain a stain
As passes coloring.

                Enter Gaoler with Emilia.

                    Dear gentlewoman,
How fares our gracious lady?

EMILIA

As well as one so great and so forlorn
May hold together. On her frights and griefs,
Which never tender lady has borne greater,
She is something before her time delivered.

PAULINA

A boy?

EMILIA A daughter, and a goodly babe,
Lusty and like to live. The queen receives
Much comfort in it, says, 'My poor prisoner,
I am innocent as you.'

PAULINA   I dare be sworn.
These fits of lunacy in the king, curse them!
He must be told of it, and he shall. The office
Becomes a woman best; I'll take it upon me.
If I prove honey-mouthed, let my tongue blister
And never to my red-looked anger be
The trumpet any more. Pray you, Emilia,
Commend my best obedience to the queen.
If she dares trust me with her little babe,
I'll show it the king and undertake to be
Her advocate to the loudest. We do not know
How he may soften at the sight of the child.
The silence often of pure innocence
Persuades when speaking fails.

EMILIA   Most worthy madam,
Your honor and your goodness are so evident
That your free undertaking cannot miss
A thriving issue. There is no lady living
So meet for this great errand. Please your ladyship
To visit the next room, I'll presently
Acquaint the queen of your most noble offer,
Who but to-day hammered of this design;

But durst not tempt a minister of honor
Lest she should be denied.

PAULINA   Tell her, Emilia,
I'll use that tongue I have. If wit flows from it
As boldness from my bosom, let it not be doubted
I shall do good.

EMILIA   Now be you blest for it!
I'll to the queen. Please you, come something nearer.

GAOLER
Madam, if it pleases the queen to send the babe,
I know not what I shall incur to pass it,
Having no warrant.

PAULINA   You need not fear it, sir.
This child was prisoner to the womb and is
By law and process of great nature thence
Freed and enfranchised; not a party to
The anger of the king nor guilty of,
If any is, the trespass of the queen.

GAOLER
I do believe it.

PAULINA
Do not you fear. Upon my honor, I
Will stand between you and danger.   *Exeunt.*

SCENE III
Leontes' palace.

Enter Leontes, Antigonus, Lords and Attendants.

LEONTES
Nor night nor day no rest. It is but weakness
To bear the matter thus—mere weakness. If
The cause were not in being—part of the cause,
She, the adulteress; for the harlot king
Is quite beyond my arm, out of the blank

And level of my brain, plot-proof. But she
I can hook to me. Say that she were gone,
Given to the fire, a moiety of my rest
Might come to me again. Who's there?
SERVANT   My lord.
LEONTES
   How does the boy?
SERVANT   He took good rest to-night.
   'Tis hoped his sickness is discharged.
LEONTES
   To see his nobleness!
   Conceiving the dishonor of his mother,
   He straight declined, drooped, took it deeply,
   Fastened and fixed the shame of it in himself,
   Threw off his spirit, his appetite, his sleep,
   And downright languished. Leave me solely. Go
   See how he fares.   *Exit Servant.*
                  Fie, fie! no thought of him!
   The very thought of my revenges that way
   Recoil upon me—in himself too mighty,
   And in his parties, his alliance. Let him be
   Until a time may serve. For present vengeance,
   Take it on her. Camillo and Polixenes
   Laugh at me, make their pastime at my sorrow.
   They should not laugh if I could reach them, nor
   Shall she within my power.

                  Enter Paulina with a Babe.

LORD   You must not enter.
PAULINA
   Nay, rather, good my lords, be second to me.
   Fear you his tyrannous passion more, alas,
   Than the queen's life? a gracious innocent soul,
   More free than he is jealous.
ANTIGONUS   That's enough.

SERVANT
    Madam, he has not slept to-night, commanded
    None should come at him.
PAULINA   Not so hot, good sir.
    I come to bring him sleep. It is such as you,
    That creep like shadows by him and do sigh
    At each his needless heavings, such as you
    Nourish the cause of his awaking. I
    Do come with words as medicinal as true,
    Honest as either, to purge him of that humor
    That presses him from sleep.
LEONTES   What noise there, ho?
PAULINA
    No noise, my lord, but needful conference
    About some godparents for your highness.
LEONTES   How?
    Away with that audacious lady! Antigonus,
    I charged you that she should not come about me.
    I knew she would.
ANTIGONUS   I told her so, my lord,
    On your displeasure's peril and on mine,
    She should not visit you.
LEONTES   What, can you not rule her?
PAULINA
    From all dishonesty he can. In this,
    Unless he takes the course that you have done,
    Commit me for committing honor, trust it,
    He shall not rule me.
ANTIGONUS   La you now, you hear!
    When she will take the rein I let her run,
    But she'll not stumble.
PAULINA   Good my liege, I come—
    And I beseech you hear me, who profess
    Myself your loyal servant, your physician,
    Your most obedient counsellor, yet that dare
    Less appear so in comforting your evils

Than such as most seem yours—I say I come
From your good queen.

LEONTES   Good queen?

PAULINA   Good queen, my lord,
Good queen. I say good queen,
And would by combat make her good, so were I
A man, the worst about you.

LEONTES   Force her hence.

PAULINA

Let him that makes but trifles of his eyes
First hand me. On my own accord I'll off,
But first I'll do my errand. The good queen,
For she is good, has brought you forth a daughter—
Here it is—commends it to your blessing.

Lays down the child.

LEONTES   Out!
A mankind witch! Hence with her, out of door!
A most intelligencing bawd.

PAULINA   Not so.
I am as ignorant in that as you
In so entitling me—and no less honest
Than you are mad; which is enough, I'll warrant,
As this world goes, to pass for honest.

LEONTES   Traitors!
Will you not push her out? Give her the bastard.
You dotard, you are woman-tired, unroosted
By your dame Partlet here. Take up the bastard.
Take it up, I say. Give it to your crone.

PAULINA   Forever
Unvenerable be your hands, if you
Take up the princess by that forcèd baseness
Which he has put upon it!

LEONTES   He dreads his wife.

PAULINA

So I would you did. Then it were past all doubt
You'd call your children yours.

LEONTES   A nest of traitors!

ANTIGONUS

I am none, by this good light.

PAULINA   Nor I, nor any
But one that's here, and that's himself; for he
The sacred honor of himself, his queen's,
His hopeful son's, his babe's, betrays to slander,
Whose sting is sharper than the sword's. And will not—
For, as the case now stands, it is a curse
He cannot be compelled to it—once remove
The root of his opinion, which is rotten
As ever oak or stone was sound.

LEONTES   A strumpet
Of boundless tongue, who late did beat her husband
And now baits me! This brat is none of mine;
It is the issue of Polixenes.
Hence with it, and together with the dam
Commit them to the fire!

PAULINA   It is yours,
And, might we lay the old proverb to your charge,
So like you 'tis the worse. Behold, my lords.
Although the print is little, the whole matter
And copy of the father—eye, nose, lip,
The trick of his frown, his forehead, nay, the valley,
The pretty dimples of its chin and cheek, its smiles,
The very mould and frame of hand, nail, finger.
And you, good goddess Nature, which have made it
So like to him that got it, if you have
The ordering of the mind too, among all colors
No yellow in it, lest she suspects, as he does,
Her children not her husband's!

LEONTES   A gross hag!
　　And, scoundrel, you are worthy to be hanged
　　That will not stay her tongue.
ANTIGONUS   Hang all the husbands
　　That cannot do that feat, you'll leave yourself
　　Hardly one subject.
LEONTES   Once more, take her hence!
PAULINA
　　A most unworthy and unnatural lord
　　Can do no more.
LEONTES   I'll have you burnt.
PAULINA   I care not.
　　It is a heretic that makes the fire,
　　Not she who burns in it. I'll not call you tyrant;
　　But this most cruel usage of your queen,
　　Not able to produce more accusation
　　Than your own weak-hinged fancy, something savors
　　Of tyranny and will ignoble make you,
　　Yes, scandalous to the world.
LEONTES   On your allegiance,
　　Out of the chamber with her! Were I a tyrant,
　　Where were her life? She durst not call me so
　　If she did know me one. Away with her!
PAULINA
　　I pray you do not push me; I'll be gone.
　　Look to your babe, my lord; 'tis yours. Jove send her
　　A better guiding spirit. What need these hands?
　　You that are thus so tender over his follies
　　Will never do him good, not one of you.
　　So, so. Farewell; we are gone.   *Exit.*
LEONTES
　　You, traitor, have set on your wife to this.
　　My child? away with it! Even you, that have
　　A heart so tender over it, take it hence
　　And see it instantly consumed with fire—
　　Even you and none but you. Take it up straight.

Within this hour bring me word it is done,
And by good testimony, or I'll seize your life,
With what you else call yours. If you refuse
And will encounter with my wrath, say so.
The bastard brains with these my very hands
Shall I dash out. Go, take it to the fire,
For you set on your wife.

ANTIGONUS   I did not, sir.
These lords, my noble fellows, if they please,
Can clear me in it.

LORDS   We can. My royal liege,
He is not guilty of her coming hither.

LEONTES
You are liars all.

LORD
Beseech your highness, give us better credit.
We have always truly served you, and beseech you
So to esteem of us; and on our knees we beg,
As recompense of our dear services
Past and to come, that you do change this purpose,
Which being so horrible, so bloody, must
Lead on to some foul issue. We all kneel.

LEONTES
I am a feather for each wind that blows.
Shall I live on to see this bastard kneel
And call me father? Better burn it now
Than curse it then. But be it; let it live.
It shall not either. You, sir, come you hither,
You that have been so tenderly officious
With Lady Margery, your midwife there,
To save this bastard's life—for 'tis a bastard,
So sure as this beard's grey. What will you adventure
To save this brat's life?

ANTIGONUS   Anything, my lord,
That my ability may undergo
And nobleness impose. At least thus much.

I'll pawn the little blood which I have left
To save the innocent. Anything possible.

LEONTES
It shall be possible. Swear by this sword
You will perform my bidding.

ANTIGONUS   I will, my lord.

LEONTES
Mark and perform it, see you; for the fail
Of any point in it shall not only be
Death to yourself but to your lewd-tongued wife,
Whom for this time we pardon. We enjoin you,
As you are liege-man to us, that you carry
This female bastard hence, and that you bear it
To some remote and desert place quite out
Of our dominions, and that there you leave it,
Without more mercy, to its own protection
And favor of the climate. As by strange fortune
It came to us, I do in justice charge you,
On your soul's peril and your body's torture,
That you commend it strangely to some place
Where chance may nurse or end it. Take it up.

ANTIGONUS
I swear to do this, though a present death
Had been more merciful. Come on, poor babe.
Some powerful spirit instruct the kites and ravens
To be your nurses. Wolves and bears, they say,
Casting their savageness aside, have done
Like offices of pity. Sir, be prosperous
In more than this deed does require. And blessing
Against this cruelty fight on your side,
Poor thing, condemned to loss.   *Exit with the Babe.*

LEONTES   No, I'll not rear
Another's issue.

Enter a Servant.

SERVANT   Please your highness, posts
    From those you sent to the oracle are come
    An hour since. Cleomenes and Dion,
    Being well arrived from Delphos, are both landed,
    Hasting to the Court.
LORD   So please you, sir, their speed
    Has been beyond account.
LEONTES   Twenty-three days
    They have been absent. 'Tis good speed, foretells
    The great Apollo suddenly will have
    The truth of this appear. Prepare you, lords;
    Summon a session, that we may arraign
    Our most disloyal lady, for, as she has
    Been publicly accused, so shall she have
    A just and open trial. While she lives
    My heart will be a burden to me. Leave me,
    And think upon my bidding.   *Exeunt.*

Act III

SCENE I
Sicilia — A road.

Enter Cleomenes and Dion.

CLEOMENES
    The climate's delicate, the air most sweet,
    Fertile the isle, the temple much surpassing
    The common praise it bears.
DION   I shall report,
    For most it caught me, the celestial habits—
    It seems I so should term them—and the reverence
    Of the grave wearers. O, the sacrifice,
    How ceremonious, solemn, and unearthly
    It was in the offering!
CLEOMENES   But of all, the burst
    And the ear-deafening voice of the oracle,
    Kin to Jove's thunder, so surprised my sense
    That I was nothing.
DION   If the event of the journey
    Proves as successful to the queen—O be it so!—
    As it has been to us rare, pleasant, speedy,
    The time is worth the use of it.
CLEOMENES   Great Apollo
    Turn all to the best! These proclamatiòns,
    So forcing faults upon Hermione,
    I little like.
DION   The violent carriage of it
    Will clear or end the business. When the oracle,
    Thus by Apollo's great divine sealed up,

Shall the contents discover, something rare
Even then will rush to knowledge. Go. Fresh horses!
And gracious be the issue!   *Exeunt.*

SCENE II
A court of justice.

Enter Leontes, Lords and Officers.

LEONTES
This sessions, to our great grief we pronounce,
Even pushes against our heart—the party tried
The daughter of a king, our wife, and one
Of us too much beloved. Let us be cleared
Of being tyrannous, since we so openly
Proceed in justice, which shall have due course,
Even to the guilt or the purgatïon.
Produce the prisoner.

OFFICER
It is his highness' pleasure that the queen
Appear in person here in court. Silence!

Enter Hermione, guarded, Paulina, and Ladies.

LEONTES
Read the indictment.

OFFICER [*reads*] Hermione, queen to the worthy Leontes,
king of Sicilia, you are here accused and arraigned of
high treason, in committing adultery with Polixenes,
king of Bohemia, and conspiring with Camillo to take
away the life of our sovereign lord the king, your royal
husband; the pretense whereof being by circumstances
partly laid open, you, Hermione, contrary to the faith
and allegiance of a true subject, did counsel and aid
them, for their better safety, to fly away by night.

HERMIONE

Since what I am to say must be but that
Which contradicts my accusation, and
The testimony on my part no other
But what comes from myself, it shall scarce help me
To say, 'Not guilty.' My integrity,
Being counted falsehood, shall, as I express it,
Be so received. But thus: if powers divine
Behold our human actions, as they do,
I doubt not then but innocence shall make
False accusation blush and tyranny
Tremble at patience. You, my lord, best know,
Who least will seem to do so, my past life
Has been as continent, as chaste, as true,
As I am now unhappy; which is more
Than history can pattern, though devised
And played to take spectators. For behold me—
A fellow of the royal bed, who own
A moiety of the throne, a great king's daughter,
The mother to a hopeful prince—here standing
To prate and talk for life and honor before
Who please to come and hear. For life, I prize it
As I weigh grief, which I would spare. For honor,
It is a derivative from me to mine,
And only that I stand for. I appeal
To your own conscience, sir, before Polixenes
Came to your Court, how I was in your grace,
How merited to be so. Since he came,
With what encounter so uncurrent I
Have strained to appear thus; if one jot beyond
The bound of honor, or in act or will
That way inclining, hardened be the hearts
Of all that hear me, and my nearest of kin
Cry fie upon my grave!

LEONTES   I never heard yet
  That any of these bolder vices wanted
  Less impudence to gainsay what they did
  Than to perform it first.
HERMIONE   That's true enough,
  Though it is a saying, sir, not due to me.
LEONTES
  You will not own it.
HERMIONE   More than mistress of
  Which comes to me in name of fault, I must not
  At all acknowledge. For Polixenes,
  With whom I am accused, I do confess
  I loved him as in honor he required—
  With such a kind of love as might become
  A lady like me, with a love even such,
  So and no other, as yourself commanded.
  Which not to have done I think had been in me
  Both disobedience and ingratitude
  To you and toward your friend, whose love had spoken,
  Even since it could speak, from an infant, freely
  That it was yours. Now, for conspiracy,
  I know not how it tastes, though it is dished
  For me to try how. All I know of it
  Is that Camillo was an honest man;
  And why he left your Court, the gods themselves,
  Knowing no more than I, are ignorant.
LEONTES
  You knew of his departure, as you know
  What you have undertaken to do in his absence.
HERMIONE
  Sir,
  You speak a language that I understand not,
  My life stands in the level of your dreams,
  Which I will lay down.

LEONTES   Your actions are my dreams.
  You had a bastard by Polixenes,
  And I but dreamed it. As you were past all shame—
  Those of your fact are so—so past all truth,
  Which to deny concerns more than avails; for as
  Your brat has been cast out, like to itself,
  No father owning it—which is, indeed,
  More criminal in you than it—so you
  Shall feel our justice, in whose easiest passage
  Look for no less than death.
HERMIONE   Sir, spare your threats.
  The threat which you would fright me with I seek.
  To me can life be no commodity.
  The crown and comfort of my life, your favor,
  I do give lost, for I do feel it gone,
  But know not how it went. My second joy
  And first-fruits of my body, from his presence
  I am barred, like one infectious. My third comfort,
  Starred most unluckily, is from my breast,
  The innocent milk in its most innocent mouth,
  Haled out to murder. Myself on every post
  Proclaimed a strumpet: with immodest hatred
  The child-bed privilege denied, which belongs
  To women of all fashion. Lastly, hurried
  Here to this place, in the open air, before
  I have got strength of limit. Now, my liege,
  Tell me what blessings I have here alive,
  That I should fear to die? Therefore proceed.
  But yet hear this—mistake me not, no life
  (I prize it not a straw) but for my honor,
  Which I would free. If I shall be condemned
  Upon surmises, all proofs sleeping else
  But what your jealousies awake, I tell you
  It is rigor and not law. Your honors all,
  I do refer me to the oracle.
  Apollo be my judge!

LORD   This your request
  Is altogether just. Therefore bring forth,
  And in Apollo's name, his oracle.

                            Exeunt certain Officers.

HERMIONE
  The emperor of Russia was my father.
  O that he were alive, and here beholding
  His daughter's trial; that he did but see
  The flatness of my misery—yet with eyes
  Of pity, not revenge.

      Enter Officers with Cleomenes, and Dion.

OFFICER
  You here shall swear upon this sword of justice,
  That you, Cleomenes and Dion, have
  Been both at Delphos, and from thence have brought
  This sealed-up oracle, by the hand delivered
  Of great Apollo's priest; and that since then
  You have not dared to break the holy seal
  Nor read the secrets in it.
CLEOMENES, DION   All this we swear.
LEONTES
  Break up the seals and read.
OFFICER [*reads*] Hermione is chaste, Polixenes blameless,
  Camillo a true subject, Leontes a jealous tyrant, his
  innocent babe truly begotten; and the king shall live
  without an heir if that which is lost be not found.
LORDS
  Now blessèd be the great Apollo!
HERMIONE   Praisèd!
LEONTES
  Have you read truth?
OFFICER   Ay, my lord, even so
  As it is here set down.

LEONTES

There is no truth at all in the oracle.

The sessions shall proceed. This is mere falsehood.

Enter Servant.

SERVANT

My lord the king, the king!

LEONTES   What is the business?

SERVANT

O sir, I shall be hated to report it.

The prince your son, with mere worry and fear

Of the queen's fate, is gone.

LEONTES   How? gone?

SERVANT   Is dead.

LEONTES

Apollo's angry, and the heavens themselves

Do strike at my injustice.

Hermione swoons.

How now there?

PAULINA

This news is mortal to the queen. Look down

And see what death is doing.

LEONTES   Take her hence.

Her heart is but overcharged; she will recover.

I have too much believed my own suspicion.

Beseech you, tenderly apply to her

Some remedies for life.

        Exeunt Paulina and Ladies with Hermione.

                    Apollo, pardon

My great profaneness against your oracle!

I will reconcile me to Polixenes,

New woo my queen, recall the good Camillo,

Whom I proclaim a man of truth, of mercy.

For, being transported by my jealousies
To bloody thoughts and to revenge, I chose
Camillo for the minister to poison
My friend Polixenes. Which had been done,
But that the good mind of Camillo tardied
My swift command; though I with death and with
Reward did threaten and encourage him,
Not doing it and being done. He, most humane
And filled with honor, to my kingly guest
Unclasped my design, quit his fortunes here,
Which you knew great; and to the hazard
Of all uncertainties himself commended,
No richer than his honor. How he glisters
Through my rust! and how his piety
Does my deeds make the blacker!

Enter Paulina.

PAULINA   Woe the while!
    O, cut my lace, lest my heart, cracking it,
    Breaks too!
LORD   What fit is this, good lady?
PAULINA
    What studied torments, tyrant, have you for me?
    What wheels? racks? fires? what flaying? boiling
    In leads or oils? what old or newer torture
    Must I receive, whose every word deserves
    To taste of your most worst? Your tyranny,
    Together working with your jealousies,
    Fancies too weak for boys, too green and idle
    For girls of nine, O, think what they have done,
    And then run mad indeed, stark mad, for all
    Your bygone fooleries were but spices of it.
    That you betrayed Polixenes, was nothing;
    That did but show you, for a fool, inconstant
    And damnably ungrateful. Nor was it much

You would have poisoned good Camillo's honor,
To have him kill a king—poor trespasses,
More monstrous standing by. Whereof I reckon
The casting forth to crows your baby daughter
To be or none or little, though a devil
Would have shed water out of fire ere done it.
Nor is it directly laid to you, the death
Of the young prince, whose honorable thoughts,
Thoughts high for one so tender, cleft the heart
That could conceive a gross and foolish sire
Blemished his gracious dam. This is not, no,
Laid to your answer. But the last—O lords,
When I have said, cry 'Woe!'—the queen, the queen,
The sweetest dear creature's dead, and vengeance for it
Not dropped down yet.

LORD   The higher powers forbid!
PAULINA

I say she's dead; I'll swear it. If word nor oath
Prevails not, go and see. If you can bring
Tincture or lustre in her lip, her eye,
Heat outwardly or breath within, I'll serve you
As I would do the gods. But, O you tyrant,
Do not repent these things, for they are heavier
Than all your woes can stir. Therefore betake you
To nothing but despair. A thousand knees
Ten thousand years together, naked, fasting,
Upon a barren mountain, and ever winter
In storm perpetual, could not move the gods
To look that way you were.

LEONTES   Go on, go on.
You can not speak too much. I have deserved
All tongues to talk their bitterest.

LORD   Say no more.
However the business goes, you have made fault
In the boldness of your speech.

PAULINA   I am sorry for it.
All faults I make, when I shall come to know them,
I do repent. Alas, I have shown too much
The rashness of a woman. He is touched
To the noble heart. What's gone and what's past help
Should be past grief. Do not receive affliction
At my petition. I beseech you, rather
Let me be punished, that reminded you
Of what you should forget. Now, good my liege,
Sir, royal sir, forgive a foolish woman.
The love I bore your queen—lo, fool again!—
I'll speak of her no more, nor of your children;
I'll not remember you of my own lord,
Who is lost too. Take your patience to you,
And I will say nothing.
LEONTES   You did speak but well
When most the truth, which I receive much better
Than to be pitied of you. Pray you, bring me
To the dead bodies of my queen and son.
One grave shall be for both. Upon them shall
The causes of their death appear, unto
Our shame perpetual. Once a day I'll visit
The chapel where they lie, and tears shed there
Shall be my recreation. So long as nature
Will bear up with this exercise, so long
I daily vow to use it. Come, and lead me
To these sorrows.   *Exeunt.*

SCENE III
Bohemia. A sea-coast.

Enter Antigonus, and a Mariner, with a Babe.

ANTIGONUS
  You are perfect then our ship has touched upon
  The deserts of Bohemia?
MARINER   Ay, my lord, and fear
  We have landed in ill time. The skies look grimly
  And threaten present blusters. In my conscience,
  The heavens with that we have in hand are angry
  And frown upon us.
ANTIGONUS
  Their sacred wills be done! Go, get aboard;
  Look to your bark. I'll not be long before
  I call upon you.
MARINER   Make your best haste, and go not
  Too far in the land. 'Tis like to be loud weather.
  Besides, this place is famous for the creatures
  Of prey that keep upon it.
ANTIGONUS   Go you away;
  I'll follow instantly.
MARINER   I am glad at heart
  To be so rid of the business.   *Exit.*
ANTIGONUS   Come, poor babe.
  I have heard, but not believed, the spirits of the dead
  May walk again. If such thing be, your mother
  Appeared to me last night, for never was dream
  So like a waking. To me comes a creature,
  Sometimes her head on one side, some another.
  I never saw a vessel of like sorrow,
  So filled and so becoming. In pure white robes,
  Like very sanctity, she did approach
  My cabin where I lay; thrice bowed before me,
  And, gasping to begin some speech, her eyes

Became two spouts. The fury spent, anon
Did this break her from: 'Good Antigonus,
Since fate, against your better disposition,
Has made your person for the thrower-out
Of my poor babe, according to your oath,
Places remote enough are in Bohemia;
There weep and leave it crying. And, since the babe
Is counted lost for ever, Perdita,
I pray you, call it. For this ungentle business,
Put on you by my lord, you never shall see
Your wife Paulina more.' And so, with shrieks,
She melted into air. Affrighted much,
I did in time collect myself, and thought
This was so and no slumber. Dreams are toys;
Yet for this once, yes, superstitiously,
I will be squared by this. I do believe
Hermione has suffered death, and that
Apollo would, this being indeed the issue
Of King Polixenes, it should here be laid,
Either for life or death, upon the earth
Of its right father. Blossom, speed you well.
There lie, and there your inscription; there these,
Which may, if fortune please, both breed you, pretty,
And still rest yours. The storm begins. Poor wretch,
That for your mother's fault are thus exposed
To loss and what may follow. Weep I cannot,
But my heart bleeds; and most accursed am I
To be by oath enjoined to this. Farewell!
The day frowns more and more. You're likely to have
A lullaby too rough. I never saw
The heavens so dim by day. A savage clamor!
Well may I get aboard! This is the chase.
I am gone for ever.   *Exit, pursued by a bear.*

Enter Shepherd.

SHEPHERD I would there were no age between ten and three-and-twenty, or that youth would sleep out the rest; for there is nothing in between but getting wenches with child, wronging the ancientry, stealing, fighting. Hark you now. Would any but these boiled brains of nineteen and two-and-twenty hunt this weather? They have scared away two of my best sheep, which I fear the wolf will sooner find than the master. If anywhere I have them, 'tis by the seaside, browsing of ivy. Good luck, if it be your will! What have we here? Mercy on us, a bairn, a very pretty bairn! A boy or a girl, I wonder? A pretty one, a very pretty one. Sure, some scape. Though I am not bookish, yet I can read waiting-gentlewoman in the scape. This has been some stair-work, some trunk-work, some behind-door-work. They were warmer that got this than the poor thing is here. I'll take it up for pity. Yet I'll tarry till my son comes. He hallooed but even now. Whoa, ho, hoa!

Enter Clown.

CLOWN Hilloa, loa!

SHEPHERD What, are you so near? If you'd see a thing to talk on when you are dead and rotten, come hither. What ails you, man?

CLOWN I have seen two such sights, by sea and by land— but I am not to say it is a sea, for it is now the sky; betwixt the firmament and it you cannot thrust a bodkin's point.

SHEPHERD Why, boy, how is it?

CLOWN I would you did but see how it chafes, how it rages, how it takes up the shore. But that's not to the point. O, the most piteous cry of the poor souls! Sometimes to see them, and not to see them. Now the ship boring the moon with her main-mast, and anon swallowed with foam and froth, as you'd thrust a cork

into a hogshead. And then for the land-service—to see
how the bear tore out his shoulder-bone, how he cried to
me for help and said his name was Antigonus, a
nobleman. But to make an end of the ship—to see how
the sea swallowed up all. But, first, how the poor souls
roared, and the sea mocked them, and how the poor
gentleman roared and the bear mocked him, both roaring
louder than the sea or weather.

SHEPHERD Name of mercy, when was this, boy?

CLOWN Now, now; I have not winked since I saw these
sights. The men are not yet cold under water, nor the
bear half dined on the gentleman. He's at it now.

SHEPHERD Would I had been by, to have helped the old
man.

CLOWN I would you had been by the ship side, to have
helped her. There your charity would have lacked
footing.

SHEPHERD Heavy matters, heavy matters! But look you
here, boy. Now bless yourself! You met with things
dying, I with things new-born. Here's a sight for you.
Look you, a christening-cloth for a squire's child. Look
you here. Take up, take up, boy; open it. So, let's see. It
was told me I should be rich by the fairies. This is some
changeling. Open it. What's within, boy?

CLOWN You're a made old man. If the sins of your youth
are forgiven you, you're well to live. Gold! all gold!

SHEPHERD This is fairy gold, boy, and it will prove so. Up
with it, keep it close. Home, home, the next way. We are
lucky, boy, and to be so always requires nothing but
secrecy. Let my sheep go. Come, good boy, the next way
home.

CLOWN Go you the next way with your findings. I'll go
see if the bear is gone from the gentleman and how
much he has eaten. They are never angry but when they
are hungry. If there is any of him left, I'll bury it.

SHEPHERD That's a good deed. If you may discern by that
 which is left of him what he is, fetch me to the sight of
 him.

CLOWN Sure, will I; and you shall help to put him in the
 ground.

SHEPHERD 'Tis a lucky day, boy, and we'll do good deeds
 of it.   *Exeunt.*

Act IV

SCENE I

Enter Time, the Chorus.

TIME
    I, that please some, try all, both joy and terror
    Of good and bad, that makes and unfolds error,
    Now take upon me, in the name of Time,
    To use my wings. Impute it not a crime
    To me or my swift passage that I slide
    Over sixteen years and leave the growth untried
    Of that wide gap, since it is in my power
    To overthrow law and in one self-born hour
    To plant and o'erwhelm custom. Let me pass
    The same I am, ere ancientest order was
    Or what is now received. I witness to
    The times that brought them in. So shall I do
    To the freshest things now reigning, and make stale
    The glistering of this present, as my tale
    Now seems to it. Your patience this allowing,
    I turn my glass and give my scene such growing
    As you had slept between. Leontes leaving,
    The effects of his mad jealousies so grieving
    That he shuts up himself, imagine me,
    Gentle spectators, that I now may be
    In fair Bohemia. And remember well,
    I mentioned a son of the king's, which Florizel
    I now name to you, and with speed so pace
    To speak of Perdita, now grown in grace
    Equal with wondering. What of her ensues

I may not prophesy; but let Time's news
Be known when 'tis brought forth. A shepherd's daughter
And what to her adheres, which follows after,
Is the argument of Time. Of this allow
If ever you have spent time worse ere now;
If never, yet that Time himself does say
He wishes earnestly you never may.   *Exit.*

SCENE II
Bohemia. Polixenes' palace.

Enter Polixenes and Camillo.

POLIXENES I pray you, good Camillo, be no more
importunate. It is a sickness denying you anything, a
death to grant this.

CAMILLO It is fifteen years since I saw my country. Though
I have for the most part been aired abroad, I desire to lay
my bones there. Besides, the penitent king, my master,
has sent for me, to whose feeling sorrows I might be
some allay—or I overween to think so—which is another
spur to my departure.

POLIXENES As you love me, Camillo, wipe not out the rest
of your services by leaving me now. The need I have of
you your own goodness has made. Better not to have had
you than thus to want you. You, having made me
businesses which none without you can sufficiently
manage, must either stay to execute them yourself or
take away with you the very services you have done.
Which if I have not enough considered—as too much I
cannot—to be more thankful to you shall be my study,
and my profit therein the heaping friendships. Of that
fatal country, Sicilia, pray speak no more, whose very
naming punishes me with the remembrance of that
penitent, as you call him, and reconciled king, my

brother; whose loss of his most precious queen and children are even now to be afresh lamented. Say to me, when saw you the Prince Florizel, my son? Kings are no less unhappy, their issue not being gracious, than they are in losing them when they have approved their virtues.

CAMILLO Sir, it is three days since I saw the prince. What his happier affairs may be are to me unknown, but I have missingly noted he is of late much retired from Court and is less frequent to his princely exercises than formerly he has appeared.

POLIXENES I have considered so much, Camillo, and with some care—so far that I have eyes under my service which look upon his removedness. From whom I have this intelligence, that he is seldom from the house of a most homely shepherd; a man, they say, that from very nothing, and beyond the imagination of his neighbors, is grown into an unspeakable estate.

CAMILLO I have heard, sir, of such a man, who has a daughter of most rare note. The report of her is extended more than can be thought to begin from such a cottage.

POLIXENES That is likewise part of my intelligence; but, I fear, the angle that plucks our son thither. You shall accompany us to the place, where we will, not appearing what we are, have some question with the shepherd. From whose simplicity I think it not uneasy to get the cause of my son's resort thither. Pray be my present partner in this business, and lay aside the thoughts of Sicilia.

CAMILLO I willingly obey your command.

POLIXENES My best Camillo! We must disguise ourselves.

Exeunt.

SCENE III
Near the Shepherd's house.

Enter Autolycus, singing.

When daffodils begin to peer,
  With heigh! the doxy over the dale,
Why, then comes in the sweet of the year,
  For the red blood reigns in the winter's pale.

The white sheet bleaching on the hedge,
  With heigh! the sweet birds, O how they sing!
Does set my thieving tooth on edge,
  For a quart of ale is a dish for a king.

The lark, that tirra-lyra chants,
  With heigh! with heigh! the thrush and the jay,
Are summer songs for me and my aunts, [girls]
  While we lie tumbling in the hay.

I have served Prince Florizel and in my time worn velvet, but now I am out of service.

But shall I go mourn for that, my dear?
  The pale moon shines by night.
And when I wander here and there,
  I then do most go right.

If tinkers may have leave to live,
  And bear the sow-skin budget,
Then my account I well may give,
  And in the stocks avouch it.

My traffic is sheets; when the kite builds, look to lesser linen. My father named me Autolycus, who being, as I am, littered under Mercury, was likewise a snapper-up of unconsidered trifles. With dice and drab I purchased this caparison, and my revenue is the silly cheat. Gallows and knock are too powerful on the highway; beating

and hanging are terrors to me. For the life to come, I
sleep out the thought of it. A prize! a prize!

Enter Clown.

CLOWN Let me see; every eleven wether tods;[1] every tod
yields pound and odd shilling; fifteen hundred shorn,
what comes the wool to?
AUTOLYCUS [*aside*]. If the springe holds, the cock's mine.
CLOWN I cannot do it without counters. Let me see; what
am I to buy for our sheep-shearing feast? Three pound
of sugar, five pound of currants, rice—what will this
sister of mine do with rice? But my father has made her
mistress of the feast, and she lays it on. She has made
me four and twenty nosegays for the shearers—three-
man songmen all, and very good ones. But they are
most of them tenors and bases, but one puritan among
them, and he sings psalms to hornpipes. I must have
saffron to color the warden pies; mace; dates?—none,
that's out of my note; nutmegs, seven; a root or two of
ginger, but that I may beg; four pound of prunes, and
as many of raisins of the sun.
AUTOLYCUS O that ever I was born!

[*Grovels on the ground.*]

CLOWN In the name of me—
AUTOLYCUS O, help me, help me! pluck but off these
rags, and then death, death!
CLOWN Alas, poor soul, you have need of more rags to lay
on you, rather than have these off.
AUTOLYCUS O, sir, the loathsomeness of them offends me
more than the stripes I have received, which are mighty
ones and millions.

---

[1]An old weight for wool.

CLOWN Alas, poor man! A million of beating may come
    to a great matter.

AUTOLYCUS I am robbed, sir, and beaten, my money and
    apparel taken from me, and these detestable things put
    upon me.

CLOWN What, by a horseman, or a footman?

AUTOLYCUS A footman, sweet sir, a footman.

CLOWN Indeed, he should be a footman by the garments
    he has left with you. If this is a horseman's coat, it has
    seen very hot service. Lend me your hand, I'll help you.
    Come, lend me your hand.

[*Helps him up.*]

AUTOLYCUS O, good sir, tenderly. O!

CLOWN Alas, poor soul!

AUTOLYCUS O, good sir, softly, good sir. I fear, sir, my
    shoulder-blade is out.

CLOWN How now? can you stand?

AUTOLYCUS [*picking his pocket*] Softly, dear sir; good sir,
    softly. You have done me a charitable office.

CLOWN Do you lack any money? I have a little money for
    you.

AUTOLYCUS No, good sweet sir; no, I beseech you, sir. I
    have a kinsman not past three quarters of a mile hence,
    unto whom I was going. I shall there have money, or
    anything I want. Offer me no money, I pray you; that
    kills my heart.

CLOWN What manner of fellow was he that robbed you?

AUTOLYCUS A fellow, sir, that I have known to go about
    with bagatelles. I knew him once a servant of the prince.
    I cannot tell, good sir, for which of his virtues it was,
    but he was certainly whipped out of the Court.

CLOWN His vices, you would say. There's no virtue whipped
    out of the Court. They cherish it to make it stay there,
    and yet it will no more but abide.

AUTOLYCUS Vices, I would say, sir. I know this man well. He has been since an ape-bearer, then a process-server, a bailiff. Then he compassed a show of the Prodigal Son, and married a tinker's wife within a mile where my land and living lie. And, having flown over many knavish professions, he settled only in rogue. Some call him Autolycus.

CLOWN Out upon him! Thief, for my life, thief! He haunts wakes, fairs, and bear-baitings.

AUTOLYCUS Very true, sir; he, sir, he. That's the rogue that put me into this apparel.

CLOWN Not a more cowardly rogue in all Bohemia. If you had but looked big and spat at him, he'd have run.

AUTOLYCUS I must confess to you, sir, I am no fighter. I am false of heart that way, and that he knew, I warrant him.

CLOWN How do you now?

AUTOLYCUS Sweet sir, much better than I was. I can stand and walk. I will even take my leave of you and pace softly towards my kinsman's.

CLOWN Shall I bring you on the way?

AUTOLYCUS No, good-faced sir; no, sweet sir.

CLOWN Then fare you well. I must go buy spices for our sheep-shearing.

AUTOLYCUS Prosper you, sweet sir.   *Exit Clown.*
Your purse is not hot enough to purchase your spice. I'll be with you at your sheep-shearing too. If I make not this cheat bring out another and the shearers prove sheep, let me be unrolled and my name put in the book of virtue.

Song.

Jog on, jog on, the foot-path way,
  And merrily take the stile-a.
A merry heart goes all the day,
  Your sad tires in a mile-a.   *Exit.*

SCENE IV
Before the Shepherd's house.

Enter Florizel and Perdita.

FLORIZEL
    These your unusual clothes to each part of you
    Do give a life—no shepherdess, but Flora
    Peering in April's front. This your sheep-shearing
    Is as a meeting of the petty gods,
    And you the queen of it.

PERDITA   Sir, my gracious lord,
    To chide at your extremes it not becomes me—
    O, pardon, that I name them. Your high self,
    The gracious mark of the land, you have obscured
    With a swain's wearing, and me, poor lowly maid,
    Most goddess-like dressed up. But that our feasts
    In every mess have folly, and the feeders
    Digest it with a custom, I should blush
    To see you so attired; swoon, I think,
    To show myself a glass.

FLORIZEL   I bless the time
    When my good falcon made her flight across
    Your father's ground.

PERDITA   Now Jove afford you cause!
    To me the difference forges dread; your greatness
    Has not been used to fear. Even now I tremble
    To think your father, by some accident,
    Should pass this way as you did. O, the Fates!
    How would he look, to see his work, so noble,
    Vilely bound up? What would he say? Or how
    Should I, in these my borrowed flaunts, behold
    The sternness of his presence?

FLORIZEL   Apprehend
    Nothing but jollity. The gods themselves,
    Humbling their deities to love, have taken

The shapes of beasts upon them. Jupiter
Became a bull, and bellowed; the green Neptune
A ram, and bleated; and the fire-robed god,
Golden Apollo, a poor humble swain,
As I seem now. Their transformatiòns
Were never for a piece of beauty rarer,
Nor in a way so chaste, since my desires
Run not before my honor, nor my lusts
Burn hotter than my faith.

PERDITA   O, but, sir,
Your resolution cannot hold when it is
Opposed, as it must be, by the power of the king.
One of these two must be necessities,
Which then will speak, that you must change this
    purpose,
Or I my life.

FLORIZEL   You dearest Perdita,
With these forced thoughts, I pray you, darken not
The mirth of the feast. Either I'll be yours, my fair,
Or not my father's. For I cannot be
My own, nor anything to any, if
I am not yours. To this I am most constant,
Though destiny says no. Be merry, gentle;
Strangle such thoughts as these with anything
That you behold the while. Your guests are coming.
Lift up your countenance, as it were the day
Of celebration of that nuptial which
We two have sworn shall come.

PERDITA   O lady Fortune,
Stand you auspicious!

FLORIZEL   See, your guests approach.
Address yourself to entertain them sprightly,
And let's be red with mirth.

*Enter Shepherd, Clown, with Polixenes,
and Camillo disguised, Mopsa, Dorcas, Servants.*

SHEPHERD
   Fie, daughter! When my old wife lived, upon
   This day she was both pantler,[2] butler, cook,
   Both dame and servant; welcomed all, served all;
   Would sing her song and dance her turn; now here
   At upper end of the table, now in the middle;
   On his shoulder, and his; her face on fire
   With labor, and the thing she took to quench it
   She would to each one sip. You are retirèd,
   As if you were a feasted one and not
   The hostess of the meeting. Pray you bid
   These unknown friends to us welcome, for it is
   A way to make us better friends, more known.
   Come, quench your blushes and present yourself
   That which you are, mistress of the feast. Come on,
   And bid us welcome to your sheep-shearing,
   As your good flock shall prosper.
PERDITA *to Polixenes*   Sir, welcome.
   It is my father's will I should take on me
   The hostess-ship of the day.

             [*To Camillo.*]

           You are welcome, sir.
   Give me those flowers there, Dorcas. Reverend sirs,
   For you there's rosemary and rue; these keep
   Seeming and savor all the winter long.
   Grace and remembrance be to you both,
   And welcome to our shearing!
POLIXENES   Shepherdess—
   A fair one are you—well you fit our ages
   With flowers of winter.

---

[2]Pantryman.

PERDITA   Sir, the year growing ancient,
    Not yet on summer's death nor on the birth
    Of trembling winter, the fairest flowers of the season
    Are our carnations and streaked gillyflowers,
    Which some call nature's bastards. Of that kind
    Our rustic garden is barren, and I care not
    To get slips of them.
POLIXENES   Wherefore, gentle maiden,
    Do you neglect them?
PERDITA   For I have heard it said
    There is an art which in their colouring shares
    With great creating nature.
POLIXENES   Say there is;
    Yet nature is made better by no means
    But nature makes that means. So, over that art,
    Which you say adds to nature, is an art
    That nature makes. You see, sweet maid, we marry
    A gentler scion to the wildest stock,
    And make conceive a bark of baser kind
    By bud of nobler race. This is an art
    Which does mend nature—change it rather—but
    The art itself is nature.
PERDITA   So it is.
POLIXENES
    Then make your garden rich in gillyflowers,
    And do not call them bastards.
PERDITA   I'll not put
    The dibble in earth to set one slip of them,
    No more than, were I painted, I would wish
    This youth should say 'twere well, and only therefore
    Desire to breed by me. Here's flowers for you,
    Hot lavender, mints, savory, marjoram,
    The marigold, that goes to bed with the sun
    And with him rises weeping. These are flowers
    Of middle summer, and I think they are given
    To men of middle age. You are very welcome.

CAMILLO
   I should leave grazing, were I of your flock,
   And only live by gazing.
PERDITA   Out, alas!
   You'd be so lean that blasts of January
   Would blow you through and through. Now, my fair
      friend,
   I would I had some flowers of the spring that might
   Become your time of day, and yours, and yours,
   That wear upon your virgin branches yet
   Your maidenheads growing. O Proserpina,
   For the flowers now that, frighted, you let fall
   From Dis's wagon; daffodils,
   That come before the swallow dares, and take
   The winds of March with beauty; violets dim,
   But sweeter than the lids of Juno's eyes
   Or Cytherea's breath; pale primroses,
   That die unmarried, ere they can behold
   Bright Phoebus in his strength—a malady
   Most incident to maids; bold oxlips and
   The crown imperial; lilies of all kinds,
   The flower-de-luce being one. O, these I lack
   To make you garlands of, and my sweet friend,
   To strew him over and over!
FLORIZEL   What, like a corpse?
PERDITA
   No, like a bank for love to lie and play on.
   Not like a corpse; or if, not to be buried,
   But alive and in my arms. Come, take your flowers.
   It seems I play as I have seen them do
   In Whitsun pastorals. Sure this robe of mine
   Does change my disposition.
FLORIZEL   What you do
   Still betters what is done. When you speak, sweet,
   I'd have you do it ever. When you sing,
   I'd have you buy and sell so, so give alms,

Pray so, and for the ordering your affairs,
To sing them too. When you do dance, I wish you
A wave of the sea, that you might ever do
Nothing but that, move still, still so,
And own no other function. Each your doing,
So singular in each particular,
Crowns what you are doing in the present deeds,
That all your acts are queens.

PERDITA   O Doricles,
Your praises are too large. But that your youth,
And the true blood which peeps fairly through it,
Do plainly give you out an unstained shepherd,
With wisdom I might fear, my Doricles,
You wooed me the false way.

FLORIZEL   I think you have
As little skill to fear as I have purpose
To put you to it. But come; our dance, I pray.
Your hand, my Perdita. So turtledoves pair
That never mean to part.

PERDITA   I'll swear for them.

POLIXENES
This is the prettiest low-born lass that ever
Ran on the greensward. Nothing she does or seems
But smacks of something greater than herself,
Too noble for this place.

CAMILLO   He tells her something
That makes her blood blush at it. Truth, she is
The queen of curds and cream.

CLOWN   Come on, strike up!

DORCAS
Mopsa must be your mistress. Surely, garlic,
To mend her kissing with!

MOPSA   Now, in good time!

CLOWN
Not a word, a word! We stand upon our manners.
Come, strike up!

Music. Here a dance of Shepherds and Shepherdesses.

POLIXENES
    Pray, good shepherd, what fair swain is this
    Who dances with your daughter?
SHEPHERD
    They call him Doricles, and boasts himself
    To have a worthy feeding. But I have it
    Upon his own report and I believe it;
    He looks honest. He says he loves my daughter.
    I think so too, for never gazed the moon
    Upon the water as he'll stand and read
    As it were my daughter's eyes; and, to be plain,
    I think there is not half a kiss to choose
    Who loves another best.
POLIXENES   She dances well.
SHEPHERD
    So she does anything, though I report it
    That should be silent. If young Doricles
    Does light upon her, she shall bring him that
    Which he not dreams of.

Enter Servant.

SERVANT O master, if you did but hear the pedlar at the
    door, you would never dance again after a drum and
    pipe—no, the bagpipe could not move you. He sings
    several tunes faster than you'll tell money. He utters
    them as he had eaten ballads and all men's ears grew to
    his tunes.
CLOWN He could never come better. He shall come in. I
    love a ballad but even too well if it is doleful matter
    merrily set down, or a very pleasant thing indeed and
    sung lamentably.
SERVANT He has songs for man or woman, of all sizes. No
    milliner can so fit his customers with gloves. He has the

prettiest love-songs for maids, so without bawdry, which
is strange, with such delicate burdens of dildos and
fadings, 'Jump her and thump her.' And where some
broad-mouthed rascal would, as it were, mean mischief
and break a foul gap into the matter, he makes the maid
to answer, 'Whoop, do me no harm, good man'; puts
him off, slights him, with 'Whoop, do me no harm,
good man.'

POLIXENES This is a brave fellow.

CLOWN Believe me, you talk of an admirable witty fellow.
Has he any unfaded wares?

SERVANT He has ribbons of all the colors in the rainbow,
points more than all the lawyers in Bohemia can
learnedly handle, though they come to him by the gross
—linens, worsteds, cambrics, lawns. Why, he sings them
over as they were gods or goddesses. You would think a
smock were a she-angel, he so chants to the sleeve-hand
and the work about the square of it.

CLOWN Pray bring him in, and let him approach singing.

PERDITA Forewarn him that he uses no scurrilous words
in his tunes.   *Exit Servant.*

CLOWN You have of these pedlars that have more in them
than you'd think, sister.

PERDITA Ay, good brother, or go about to think.

Enter Autolycus, singing.

    Lawn as white as driven snow,
    Cyprus black as ever was crow;
    Gloves as sweet as damask roses,
    Masks for faces and for noses;
    Beaded bracelet, necklace amber,
    Perfume for a lady's chamber;
    Golden quoifs and stomachers
    For my lads to give their dears;
    Pins and poking-sticks of steel,

What maids lack from head to heel.
Come buy of me, come; come buy, come buy.
Buy, lads, or else your lasses cry.
Come buy.

CLOWN If I were not in love with Mopsa, you should take
no money of me; but being enthralled as I am, it will
also be the bondage of certain ribbons and gloves.

MOPSA I was promised them against the feast, but they
come not too late now.

DORCAS He has promised you more than that, or there are
liars.

MOPSA He has paid you all he promised you. May be he has
paid you more, which will shame you to give him again.

CLOWN Are there no manners left among maids? Will
they wear their aprons where they should bear their
faces? Is there not milking-time, when you are going to
bed, or kiln-hole, to whistle off these secrets, but you
must be tittle-tattling before all our guests? 'Tis well
they are whispering. Run down your tongues, and not a
word more.

MOPSA I have done. Come, you promised me a coloured
kerchief and a pair of sweet gloves.

CLOWN Have I not told you how I was cozened by the way
and lost all my money?

AUTOLYCUS And indeed, sir, there are cozeners abroad;
therefore it behoves men to be wary.

CLOWN Fear not you, man; you shall lose nothing here.

AUTOLYCUS I hope so, sir, for I have about me many
parcels of value.

CLOWN What have you here? Ballads?

MOPSA Pray now, buy some. I love a ballad in print, on
my life, for then we are sure they are true.

AUTOLYCUS Here's one to a very doleful tune, how a
usurer's wife was brought to bed of twenty money-bags
at a burden, and how she longed to eat adders' heads
and toads grilled.

MOPSA Is it true, think you?

AUTOLYCUS Very true, and but a month old.

DORCAS Bless me from marrying a usurer!

AUTOLYCUS Here's the midwife's name to it, one Mistress
   Tale-porter, and five or six honest wives that were present.
   Why should I carry lies abroad?

MOPSA Pray you now, buy it.

CLOWN Come on, lay it by. And let's first see more ballads;
   we'll buy the other things anon.

AUTOLYCUS Here's another ballad of a fish that appeared
   upon the coast on Wednesday the fourscore of April,
   forty thousand fathom above water, and sung this ballad
   against the hard hearts of maids. It was thought she was
   a woman and was turned into a cold fish, for she would
   not exchange flesh with one that loved her. The ballad
   is very pitiful and as true.

DORCAS Is it true too, think you?

AUTOLYCUS Five justices' hands at it, and witnesses more
   than my pack will hold.

CLOWN Lay it by too. Another.

AUTOLYCUS This is a merry ballad, but a very pretty one.

MOPSA Let's have some merry ones.

AUTOLYCUS Why, this is a passing merry one and goes to
   the tune of 'Two maids wooing a man.' There's scarce a
   maid westward but she sings it. 'Tis in request, I can
   tell you.

MOPSA We can both sing it; if you'll bear a part, you shall
   hear. 'Tis in three parts.

DORCAS We had the tune of it a month ago.

AUTOLYCUS I can bear my part; you must know it is my
   occupation. Have at it with you.

Song.

AUTOLYCUS Get you hence, for I must go
                        Where it fits not you to know.
DORCAS   Whither?
MOPSA   O, whither?
DORCAS   Whither?
MOPSA   It becomes your oath full well,
                        You to me your secrets tell.
DORCAS   Me too; let me go thither.
MOPSA   Either you go to the grange or mill.
DORCAS   If to either, you do ill.
AUTOLYCUS Neither.
DORCAS   What, neither?
AUTOLYCUS   Neither.
DORCAS   You have sworn my love to be.
MOPSA   You have sworn it more to me.
                        Then whither go? say, whither?

CLOWN We'll have this song out anon by ourselves. My
    father and the gentlemen are in serious talk, and we'll
    not trouble them. Come, bring away your pack after me.
    Wenches, I'll buy for you both. Pedlar, let's have the first
    choice. Follow me, girls.

                                    Exit with Dorcas and Mopsa.
AUTOLYCUS And you shall pay well for them.

                        Follows singing.

                              Song.

                              Will you buy any tape,
                  Or lace for your cape,
                My dainty duck, my dear-a?
                      Any silk, any thread,
                      Any toys for your head
                Of the newest and finest, wear-a?

Come to the pedlar.
Money's a meddler
That does sell all men's ware-a.   *Exit.*

Enter Servant.

SERVANT Master, there are three carters, three shepherds,
three cowherds, three swineherds, that have made
themselves all men of hair. They call themselves Satyrs,
and they have a dance which the wenches say is a hodge-
podge of gambols, because they are not in it. But they
themselves are of the mind, if it is not too rough for some
that know little but bowling, it will please plentifully.

SHEPHERD Away! we'll none of it. Here has been too much
homely foolery already. I know, sir, we weary you.

POLIXENES You weary those that refresh us. Pray, let's see
these four threes of herdsmen.

SERVANT One three of them, by their own report, sir, has
danced before the king; and not the worst of the three
but jumps twelve foot and a half by the square.

SHEPHERD Leave your prating. Since these good men are
pleased, let them come in; but quickly now.

SERVANT Why, they stay at door, sir.   *Exit.*

Here a dance of twelve Satyrs, and exeunt.

POLIXENES
O, father, you'll know more of that hereafter.

[*To Camillo.*]

Is it not too far gone? 'Tis time to part them.
He's simple and tells much.—How now, fair shepherd,
Your heart is full of something that does take
Your mind from feasting. True, when I was young
And handed love as you do, I was wont

To load my she with knacks. I would have ransacked
The pedlar's silken treasury and have poured it
To her acceptance. You have let him go
And nothing traded with him. If your lass
Interpretation should abuse and call this
Your lack of love or bounty, you were straited
For a reply—at least if you make a care
Of happy holding her.

FLORIZEL   Old sir, I know
She prizes not such trifles as these are.
The gifts she looks from me are packed and locked
Up in my heart, which I have given already,
But not delivered. O, hear me breathe my life
Before this ancient sir, who, it should seem,
Has sometime loved. I take your hand, this hand
As soft as dove's down and as white as it,
Or Ethiopian's tooth, or the fanned snow that's sifted
By the northern blasts twice over.

POLIXENES   What follows this?
How prettily the young swain seems to wash
The hand that was fair before! I have put you out.
But to your protestation; let me hear
What you profess.

FLORIZEL   Do, and be witness to it.

POLIXENES
And this my neighbor too?

FLORIZEL   And he, and more
Than he, and men, the earth, the heavens, and all—
That, were I crowned the most imperial monarch,
Thereof most worthy, were I the fairest youth
That ever made eye swerve, had force and knowledge
More than was ever man's, I would not prize them
Without her love. For her employ them all;
Commend them and condemn them to her service
Or to their own perdition.

POLIXENES   Fairly offered.

CAMILLO
  This shows a sound affection.
SHEPHERD   But, my daughter,
  Say you the like to him?
PERDITA   I cannot speak
  So well, nothing so well; no, nor mean better.
  By the pattern of my own thoughts I cut out
  The purity of his.
SHEPHERD   Take hands, a bargain!
  And, friends unknown, you shall bear witness to it.
  I give my daughter to him and will make
  Her portion equal his.
FLORIZEL   O, that must be
  In the virtue of your daughter. One being dead,
  I shall have more than you can dream of yet,
  Enough then for your wonder. But, come on,
  Contract us before these witnesses.
SHEPHERD   Come, your hand;
  And, daughter, yours.
POLIXENES   Soft, swain, awhile, beseech you.
  Have you a father?
FLORIZEL   I have, but what of him?
POLIXENES
  Knows he of this?
FLORIZEL   He neither does nor shall.
POLIXENES
  I think a father
  Is at the nuptials of his son a guest
  That best becomes the table. Pray you once more,
  Is not your father grown incapable
  Of reasonable affairs? Is he not stupid
  With age and altering ills? Can he speak? hear?
  Know man from man? dispute his own estate?
  Lies he not bed-ridden? and again does nothing
  But what he did being childish?

FLORIZEL   No, good sir,
  He has his health and ampler strength indeed
  Than most have of his age.
POLIXENES   By my white beard,
  You offer him, if this is so, a wrong
  Something unfilial. Reason my son
  Should choose himself a wife; but as good reason
  The father, all whose joy is nothing else
  But fair posterity, should hold some counsel
  In such a business.
FLORIZEL   I yield all this;
  But for some other reasons, my grave sir,
  Which it is not fit you know, I not acquaint
  My father of this business.
POLIXENES   Let him know it.
FLORIZEL
  He shall not.
POLIXENES Pray you, let him.
FLORIZEL   No, he must not.
SHEPHERD
  Let him, my son. He shall not need to grieve
  At knowing of your choice.
FLORIZEL   Come, come, he must not.
  Mark our contract.
POLIXENES   Mark your divorce, young sir,

Discovers himself.

  Whom son I dare not call. You art too base
  To be acknowledged. You a sceptre's heir,
  That thus affects a sheep-hook!—You old traitor,
  I am sorry that by hanging you I can
  But shorten your life one week.—And you, fresh piece
  Of excellent witchcraft, who of force must know
  The royal fool you cope with—
SHEPHERD   O, my heart!

POLIXENES
  I'll have your beauty scratched with briers, and made
  More homely than your state.—For you, foolish boy,
  If I may ever know you do but sigh
  That you no more shall see this toy—as never
  I mean you shall—we'll bar you from succession,
  Not hold you of our blood, no, not our kin,
  Far than Deucalion off. Mark you my words.
  Follow us to the Court.—You churl, for this time,
  Though full of our displeasure, yet we free you
  From the dead blow of it.—And you, enchantment,
  Worthy enough a herdsman—yes, him too,
  That makes himself, but for our honor therein,
  Unworthy you—if ever henceforth you
  These rural latches to his entrance open,
  Or hoop his body more with your embraces,
  I will devise a death as cruel for you
  As you are tender to it.   *Exit.*

PERDITA   Even here undone!
  I was not much afraid; for once or twice
  I was about to speak and tell him plainly
  The selfsame sun that shines upon his Court
  Hides not his visage from our cottage, but
  Looks on alike. Will it please you, sir, be gone?
  I told you what would come of this. Beseech you,
  Of your own state take care. This dream of mine—
  Being now awake, I'll queen it no inch farther,
  But milk my ewes and weep.

CAMILLO   Why, how now, father?
  Speak ere you die.

SHEPHERD   I cannot speak, nor think,
  Nor dare to know that which I know. O sir,
  You have undone a man of fourscore three,
  That thought to fill his grave in quiet, yes,
  To die upon the bed my father died,
  To lie close by his honest bones. But now

Some hangman must put on my shroud and lay me
Where no priest shovels in dust. O cursèd wretch,
That knew this was the prince, and would adventure
To mingle faith with him. Undone! undone!
If I might die within this hour, I have lived
To die when I desire.   *Exit.*

FLORIZEL   Why look you so upon me?
  I am but sorry, not afraid; delayed,
  But nothing altered. What I was, I am,
  More straining on for plucking back, not following
  My leash unwillingly.

CAMILLO   Gracious my lord,
  You know your father's temper. At this time
  He will allow no speech, which I do guess
  You do not purpose to him; and as hardly
  Will he endure your sight as yet, I fear.
  Then, till the fury of his highness settles,
  Come not before him.

FLORIZEL   I do not purpose it.
  I think—Camillo?

CAMILLO   Even he, my lord.

PERDITA
  How often have I told you it would be thus?
  How often said my dignity would last
  But till it were known!

FLORIZEL   It cannot fail but by
  The violation of my faith; and then
  Let nature crush the sides of the earth together
  And mar the seeds within. Lift up your looks.
  From my succession wipe me, father. I
  Am heir to my affection.

CAMILLO   Be advised.

FLORIZEL
  I am, and by my fancy. If my reason
  Will thereto be obedient, I have reason;

If not, my senses, better pleased with madness,
Do bid it welcome.

CAMILLO   This is desperate, sir.

FLORIZEL
So call it, but it does fulfil my vow.
I needs must think it honesty. Camillo,
Not for Bohemia nor the pomp that may
Be thereat gleaned, for all the sun sees or
The close earth wombs or the profound seas hide
In unknown fathoms, will I break my oath
To this my fair beloved. Therefore, I pray you,
As you have ever been my father's honored friend,
When he shall miss me—as, in faith, I mean not
To see him any more—cast your good counsels
Upon his passion. Let myself and fortune
Tug for the time to come. This you may know
And so deliver: I am put to sea
With her whom here I cannot hold on shore.
And most opportune to our need I have
A vessel rides fast by, but not prepared
For this design. What course I mean to hold
Shall nothing benefit your knowledge, nor
Concern me the reporting.

CAMILLO   O my lord,
I would your spirit were easier for advice
Or stronger for your need.

FLORIZEL   Hark, Perdita.

Draws her aside.

I'll hear you by and by.

CAMILLO   He's irremovable,
Resolved for flight. Now were I happy if
His going I could frame to serve my turn;
Save him from danger, do him love and honor;
Purchase the sight again of dear Sicilia

And that unhappy king, my master, whom
I so much thirst to see.

FLORIZEL   Now, good Camillo.
I am so fraught with weighty business that
I leave out ceremony.

CAMILLO   Sir, I think
You have heard of my poor services in the love
That I have borne your father?

FLORIZEL   Very nobly
Have you deserved. It is my father's music
To speak your deeds, not little of his care
To have them recompensed as thought on.

CAMILLO   Well, my lord,
If you may please to think I love the king
And, through him, what's nearest to him, which is
Your gracious self, embrace but my direction.
If your more ponderous and settled project
May suffer alteration, on my honor,
I'll point you where you shall have such receiving
As shall become your highness. Where you may
Enjoy your mistress, from whom, I see indeed,
There's no disjunction to be made but by—
As heavens forfend!—your ruin; marry her,
And, with my best endeavors in your absence,
Your discontenting father strive to qualify
And bring him up to liking.

FLORIZEL   How, Camillo,
May this, almost a miracle, be done?
That I may call you something more than man,
And after that trust to you.

CAMILLO   Have you thought on
A place whereto you will go?

FLORIZEL   Not any yet.
But as the unthought-on accident is guilty
To what we wildly do, so we profess

Ourselves to be the slaves of chance, and flies
Of every wind that blows.
CAMILLO   Then listen to me.
This follows: if you will not change your purpose
But undergo this flight, make for Sicilia,
And there present yourself and your fair princess,
For so I see she must be, before Leontes.
She shall be habited as it becomes
The partner of your bed. I think I see
Leontes opening his free arms and weeping
His welcome forth; asks you the son forgiveness,
As 'twere in the father's person; kisses the hands
Of your fresh princess; over and over divides him
Between his unkindness and his kindness. The one
He chides to hell and bids the other grow
Faster than thought or time.
FLORIZEL   Worthy Camillo,
What color for my visitation shall I
Hold up before him?
CAMILLO   Sent by the king your father
To greet him and to give him comfort. Sir,
The manner of your bearing towards him, with
What you, as from your father, shall deliver,
Things known betwixt us three, I'll write you down.
That shall point you forth at every sitting
What you must say, that he shall not perceive
But that you have your father's bosom there
And speak his very heart.
FLORIZEL   I am bound to you.
There is some sap in this.
CAMILLO   A course more promising
Than a wild dedication of yourselves
To unpathed waters, undreamed shores, most certain
To miseries enough. No hope to help you,
But as you shake off one to take another;
Nothing so certain as your anchors, which

Do their best office if they can but stay you
Where you'll be loath to be. Besides, you know
Prosperity is the very bond of love,
Whose fresh complexion and whose heart together
Affliction alters.

PERDITA   One of these is true.
I think affliction may subdue the cheek
But not take in the mind.

CAMILLO   Yea, say you so?
There shall not at your father's house these seven years
Be born another such.

FLORIZEL   My good Camillo,
She is as forward of her breeding as
She is in the rear of your birth.

CAMILLO   I cannot say
She lacks instruction, for she seems a mistress
To most that teach.

PERDITA   Your pardon, sir. For this
I'll blush you thanks.

FLORIZEL   My prettiest Perdita!
But O, the thorns we stand upon! Camillo,
Preserver of my father, now of me,
The medicine of our house, how shall we do?
We are not furnished like Bohemia's son,
Nor shall appear in Sicilia.

CAMILLO   My lord,
Fear none of this. I think you know my fortunes
Do all lie there. It shall be so my care
To have you royally appointed as if
The scene you play were mine. For instance, sir,
That you may know you shall not want, one word.

They talk aside. Enter Autolycus.

AUTOLYCUS Ha, ha, what a fool Honesty is! and Trust, his
sworn brother, a very simple gentleman! I have sold all

my trumpery. Not a counterfeit stone, not a ribbon,
glass, pomander, brooch, table-book, ballad, knife, tape,
glove, shoe-tie, bracelet, horn-ring, to keep my pack
from fasting. They throng who should buy first, as if
my trinkets had been hallowed and brought a benediction
to the buyer; by which means I saw whose purse was
best in picture, and what I saw, to my good use I
remembered. My clown, who wants but something to
be a reasonable man, grew so in love with the wenches'
song that he would not stir his toes till he had both tune
and words, which so drew the rest of the herd to me that
all their other senses stuck in ears. You might have
pinched a petticoat, it was senseless; 'twas nothing to
geld a codpiece of a purse; I would have filed keys off
that hung in chains. No hearing, no feeling, but my
sir's song and admiring the nothing of it. So that in this
time of lethargy I picked and cut most of their festival
purses; and had not the old man come in with a hub-
bub against his daughter and the king's son and scared
my choughs from the chaff, I had not left a purse alive
in the whole army.

Camillo, Florizel, and Perdita come forward.

CAMILLO
    Nay, but my letters, by this means being there
    So soon as you arrive, shall clear that doubt.
FLORIZEL
    And those that you shall procure from King Leontes—
CAMILLO
    Shall satisfy your father.
PERDITA   Happy be you!
    All that you speak shows fair.
CAMILLO [*seeing Autolycus*] Whom have we here?
    We'll make an instrument of this, omit
    Nothing may give us aid.

AUTOLYCUS If they have overheard me now, why, hanging.

CAMILLO
How now, good fellow? Why shake you so?
Fear not, man; here's no harm intended to you.

AUTOLYCUS I am a poor fellow, sir.

CAMILLO Why, be so ever; here's nobody will steal that
from you. Yet for the outside of your poverty we must
make an exchange. Therefore undress instantly—you
must think there's a necessity in it—and change garments
with this gentleman. Though the pennyworth on his
side is the worse, yet hold you, there's some help.

AUTOLYCUS I am a poor fellow, sir. [aside] I know you well
enough.

CAMILLO Nay, pray, dispatch. The gentleman is half flayed
already.

AUTOLYCUS Are you in earnest, sir? [aside] I smell the
trick of it.

FLORIZEL Dispatch, I pray.

AUTOLYCUS Indeed, I have had earnest, but I cannot with
conscience take it.

CAMILLO Unbuckle, unbuckle.

[Florizel and Autolycus exchange garments.]

Fortunate mistress—let my prophecy
Come home to you!—you must retire yourself
Into some covert. Take your sweetheart's hat
And pluck it over your brows, muffle your face,
Dismantle you and, as you can, disliken
The truth of your own seeming, that you may—
For I do fear eyes over—to shipboard
Get undescried.

PERDITA   I see the play so lies
That I must bear a part.

CAMILLO   No remedy.
Have you done there?

FLORIZEL   Should I now meet my father,
  He would not call me son.
CAMILLO   Nay, you shall have no hat.
                     Gives it to Perdita.
  Come, lady, come. Farewell, my friend.
AUTOLYCUS   Adieu, sir.
FLORIZEL
  O Perdita, what have we twain forgotten?
  Pray you, a word.
CAMILLO [*aside*]
  What I do next, shall be to tell the king
  Of this escape and whither they are bound.
  Wherein my hope is I shall so prevail
  To force him after; in whose company
  I shall review Sicilia, for whose sight
  I have a woman's longing.
FLORIZEL   Fortune speed us!
  Thus we set on, Camillo, to the seaside.
CAMILLO
  The swifter speed the better.
          Exeunt Florizel, Perdita, and Camillo.
AUTOLYCUS I understand the business, I hear it. To have
  an open ear, a quick eye, and a nimble hand is necessary
  for a cutpurse. A good nose is requisite also, to smell out
  work for the other senses. I see this is the time that the
  unjust man does thrive. What an exchange had this
  been without profit! What profit is here with this
  exchange! Sure the gods do this year connive at us, and
  we may do any thing extempore. The prince himself is
  about a piece of iniquity, stealing away from his father
  with his clog at his heels. If I thought it were a piece of
  honesty to acquaint the king with it, I would not do it. I
  hold it the more knavery to conceal it, and therein am I
  constant to my profession.

        Enter Clown and Shepherd.

Aside, aside! Here is more matter for a hot brain. Every
lane's end, every shop, church, session, hanging, yield a
careful man work.

CLOWN See, see! What a man you are now! There is no
other way but to tell the king she's a changeling and
none of your flesh and blood.

SHEPHERD Nay, but hear me.

CLOWN Nay, but hear me.

SHEPHERD Go to, then.

CLOWN She being none of your flesh and blood, your
flesh and blood has not offended the king, and so your
flesh and blood is not to be punished by him. Show
those things you found about her, those secret things,
all but what she has with her. This being done, let the
law go whistle, I warrant you.

SHEPHERD I will tell the king all, every word—yes, and
his son's pranks too, who, I may say, is no honest man,
neither to his father nor to me, to go about to make me
the king's brother-in-law.

CLOWN Indeed, brother-in-law was the farthest off you
could have been to him, and then your blood had been
the dearer by I know how much an ounce.

AUTOLYCUS [aside] Very wisely, puppies.

SHEPHERD Well, let us to the king. There is that in this
bundle will make him scratch his beard.

AUTOLYCUS [aside] I know not what impediment this
complaint may be to the flight of my master.

CLOWN Pray heartily he be at the palace.

AUTOLYCUS [aside] Though I am not naturally honest,
I am so sometimes by chance. Let me pocket up my
pedlar's excrement. [Takes off his false beard.] How
now, rustics, whither are you bound?

SHEPHERD To the palace, if it likes your worship.

AUTOLYCUS Your affairs, there, what, with whom, the
condition of that bundle, the place of your dwelling,

your names, your ages, of what having, breeding, and
anything that is fitting to be known, discover.

CLOWN We are but plain fellows, sir.

AUTOLYCUS A lie! You are rough and hairy. Let me have
no lying. It becomes none but tradesmen, and they
often give us soldiers the lie; but we pay them for it with
stamped coin, not stabbing steel; therefore they do not
give us the lie.

CLOWN Your worship had like to have given us one, if
you had not taken yourself with the manner.

SHEPHERD Are you a courtier, if it likes you, sir?

AUTOLYCUS Whether it likes me or no, I am a courtier.
See you not the air of the Court in these enfoldings?
Has not my gait in it the measure of the Court? Receives
not your nose Court-odor from me? Reflect I not on
your baseness, Court-contempt? Think you, because I
insinuate, or tease from you your business, I am therefore
no courtier? I am courtier head to foot, and one that
will either push on or pluck back your business there.
Whereupon I command you to open your affair.

SHEPHERD My business, sir, is to the king.

AUTOLYCUS What advocate have you to him?

SHEPHERD I know not, if it likes you.

CLOWN Advocate's the court-word for a pheasant. Say you
have none.

SHEPHERD None, sir. I have no pheasant, cock nor hen.

AUTOLYCUS

How blessèd are we that are not simple men!
Yet nature might have made me as these are;
Therefore I will not disdain.

CLOWN This cannot be but a great courtier.

SHEPHERD His garments are rich, but he wears them not
handsomely.

CLOWN He seems to be the more noble in being fantastical.
A great man, I'll warrant. I know by the picking of his
teeth.

AUTOLYCUS The bundle there? What's in the bundle? Wherefore that box?

SHEPHERD Sir, there lie such secrets in this bundle and box, which none must know but the king, and which he shall know within this hour if I may come to the speech of him.

AUTOLYCUS Age, you have lost your labor.

SHEPHERD Why, sir?

AUTOLYCUS The king is not at the palace. He is gone aboard a new ship to purge melancholy and air himself; for, if you are capable of things serious, you must know the king is full of grief.

SHEPHERD So 'tis said, sir—about his son, that should have married a shepherd's daughter.

AUTOLYCUS If that shepherd is not in custody, let him fly. The curses he shall have, the tortures he shall feel, will break the back of man, the heart of monster.

CLOWN Think you so, sir?

AUTOLYCUS Not he alone shall suffer what wit can make heavy and vengeance bitter; but those that are germane to him, though removed fifty times, shall all come under the hangman—which, though it is great pity, yet it is necessary. An old sheep-whistling rogue, a ram-tender, to offer to have his daughter come into grace! Some say he shall be stoned, but that death is too soft for him, say I. Draw our throne into a sheep-cote! All deaths are too few, the sharpest too easy.

CLOWN Has the old man ever a son, sir, do you hear, if it likes you, sir?

AUTOLYCUS He has a son, who shall be flayed alive; then anointed over with honey, set on the head of a wasp's nest; then stand till he is three quarters and a dram dead; then recovered again with aqua-vitae or some other hot infusion. Then, raw as he is, and in the hottest day prognostication proclaims, shall he be set against a brick-wall, the sun looking with a southward

eye upon him, where it is to behold him with flies
blown to death. But what talk we of these traitorly
rascals, whose miseries are to be smiled at, their offenses
being so capital? Tell me, for you seem to be honest
plain men, what you have to the king. Being something
gently considered, I'll bring you where he is aboard,
tender your persons to his presence, whisper him in
your behalfs; and if it is in man besides the king to
effect your suits, here is man shall do it.

CLOWN He seems to be of great authority. Close with him,
give him gold; and though authority is a stubborn bear,
yet he is oft led by the nose with gold. Show the inside
of your purse to the outside of his hand, and no more
ado. Remember 'stoned,' and 'flayed alive.'

SHEPHERD If it pleases you, sir, to undertake the business
for us, here is that gold I have. I'll make it as much more
and leave this young man in pawn till I bring it you.

AUTOLYCUS After I have done what I promised?

SHEPHERD Ay, sir.

AUTOLYCUS Well, give me the moiety. Are you a party in
this business?

CLOWN In some sort, sir. But though my case is a pitiful
one, I hope I shall not be flayed out of it.

AUTOLYCUS O, that's the case of the shepherd's son. Hang
him, he'll be made an example.

CLOWN Comfort, good comfort! We must to the king and
show our strange sights. He must know it is none of
your daughter nor my sister; we are gone else. Sir, I will
give you as much as this old man does when the business
is performed, and remain, as he says, your pawn till it
is brought you.

AUTOLYCUS I will trust you. Walk before toward the seaside.
Go on the right hand. I will but look upon the hedge
and follow you.

CLOWN We are blest in this man, as I may say, even blest.

SHEPHERD Let's before as he bids us. He was provided to
    do us good.   *Exeunt Shepherd and Clown.*
AUTOLYCUS If I had a mind to be honest, I see Fortune
    would not suffer me; she drops booties in my mouth. I
    am courted now with a double occasion, gold and a
    means to do the prince my master good, which who
    knows how that may turn back to my advancement? I
    will bring these two moles, these blind ones, aboard
    him. If he thinks it fit to shore them again and that the
    complaint they have to the king concerns him nothing,
    let him call me rogue for being so far officious; for I am
    proof against that title and what shame else belongs to
    it. To him will I present them; there may be matter in it.
                                                    Exit.

Act V

❀

SCENE I
Sicilia. Leontes' palace.

Enter Leontes, Cleomenes, Dion, Paulina, Servants.

CLEOMENES
Sir, you have done enough, and have performed
A saint-like sorrow. No fault could you make
Which you have not redeemed—indeed, paid down
More penitence than done trespass. At the last,
Do as the heavens have done, forget your evil;
With them forgive yourself.

LEONTES   While I remember
Her and her virtues, I cannot forget
My blemishes in them, and so still think of
The wrong I did myself, which was so much
That heirless it has made my kingdom and
Destroyed the sweetest companion ever man
Bred his hopes out of.

PAULINA   True, too true, my lord.
If one by one you wedded all the world,
Or from the all that are took something good
To make a perfect woman, she you killed
Would be unparalleled.

LEONTES   I think so. Killed?
She I killed? I did so, but you strike me
Sorely to say I did. It is as bitter
Upon your tongue as in my thought. Now, good now,
Say so but seldom.

CLEOMENES   Not at all, good lady.
   You might have spoken a thousand things that would
   Have done the time more benefit and graced
   Your kindness better.
PAULINA   You are one of those
   Would have him wed again.
DION   If you would not so,
   You pity not the state nor the remembrance
   Of his most sovereign name, consider little
   What dangers, by his highness' fail of issue,
   May drop upon his kingdom and devour
   Uncertain lookers-on. What were more holy
   Than to rejoice the former queen is well?
   What holier than, for royalty's repair,
   For present comfort and for future good,
   To bless the bed of majesty again
   With a sweet fellow to it?
PAULINA   There is none worthy,
   Respecting her that's gone. Besides, the gods
   Will have fulfilled their secret purposes;
   For has not the divine Apollo said,
   Is it not the tenor of his oracle,
   That King Leontes shall not have an heir
   Till his lost child is found? Which that it shall
   Is all as monstrous to our human reason
   As my Antigonus to break his grave
   And come again to me, who, on my life,
   Did perish with the infant. It is your counsel
   My lord should to the heavens be contrary,
   Oppose against their wills.

[To Leontes.]

            Care not for issue;
The crown will find an heir. Great Alexander

Left his to the worthiest; so his successor
Was like to be the best.

LEONTES   Good Paulina,
Who have the memory of Hermione,
I know, in honor, O that ever I
Had squared me to your counsel! Then even now
I might have looked upon my queen's full eyes,
Have taken treasure from her lips—

PAULINA   And left them
More rich for what they yielded.

LEONTES   You speak truth.
No more such wives; therefore, no wife! One worse,
And better used, would make her sainted spirit
Again possess her corpse, and on this stage,
Where we offend as now, appear soul-vexed,
And begin, 'Why to me?'

PAULINA   Had she such power,
She had just cause.

LEONTES   She had, and would incense me
To murder her I married.

PAULINA   I should so.
Were I the ghost that walked, I'd bid you mark
Her eye, and tell me for what dull part in it
You chose her. Then I'd shriek, that even your ears
Should rift to hear me, and the words that followed
Should be 'Remember mine.'

LEONTES   Stars, stars,
And all eyes else dead coals! Fear you no wife;
I'll have no wife, Paulina.

PAULINA   Will you swear
Never to marry but by my free leave?

LEONTES
Never, Paulina, so be blest my spirit.

PAULINA
Then, good my lords, bear witness to his oath.

CLEOMENES
　You tempt him overmuch.
PAULINA　　　　　　　Unless another,
　As like Hermione as is her picture,
　Affronts his eye.
CLEOMENES　　Good madam—
PAULINA　　　　　　　I have done.
　Yet, if my lord will marry—if you will, sir,
　No remedy but you will—give me the office
　To choose you a queen. She shall not be so young
　As was your former, but she shall be such
　As, walked your first queen's ghost, it should take joy
　To see her in your arms.
LEONTES　　　　　　My true Paulina,
　We shall not marry till you bid us.
PAULINA　　　　　　　　That
　Shall be when your first queen is again in breath.
　Never till then.

Enter a Servant.

SERVANT
　One that gives out himself Prince Florizel,
　Son of Polixenes, with his princess—she
　The fairest I have yet beheld—desires access
　To your high presence.
LEONTES　　　　　　What with him? He comes not
　Like to his father's greatness. His approach,
　So out of circumstance and sudden, tells us
　It is not a visitation framed, but forced
　By need and accident. What train?
SERVANT　　　　　　　　But few,
　And those but mean.
LEONTES　　　His princess, say you, with him?

SERVANT
    Ay, the most peerless piece of earth, I think,
    That ever the sun shone bright on.
PAULINA   O Hermione.
    As every present time does boast itself
    Above a better gone, so must your grave
    Give way to what's seen now. Sir, you yourself
    Have said and written so, but your writing now
    Is colder than that theme. She had not been,
    And was not to be equalled—thus your verse
    Flowed with her beauty once. 'Tis shrewdly ebbed
    To say you have seen a better.
SERVANT   Pardon, madam.
    The one I have almost forgotten—your pardon;
    The other, when she has obtained your eye,
    Will have your tongue too. This is a creature,
    Would she begin a sect, might quench the zeal
    Of all professors else, make proselytes
    Of whom she but bid follow.
PAULINA   How? not women?
SERVANT
    Women will love her that she is a woman
    More worth than any man; men, that she is
    The rarest of all women.
LEONTES   Go, Cleomenes.
    Yourself, assisted with your honored friends,
    Bring them to our embracement.
                   Exit Cleomenes with others.
                  Still, it is strange
    He thus should steal upon us.
PAULINA   Had our prince,
    Jewel of children, seen this hour, he had paired
    Well with this lord. There was not full a month
    Between their births.

LEONTES   Pray, no more; cease. You know
  He dies to me again when talked of. Sure,
  When I shall see this gentleman, your speeches
  Will bring me to consider that which may
  Unfurnish me of reason. They are come.

   Enter Florizel, Perdita, Cleomenes, and others.

  Your mother was most true to wedlock, prince,
  For she did print your royal father off,
  Conceiving you. Were I but twenty-one,
  Your father's image is so hit in you,
  His very air, that I should call you brother,
  As I did him, and speak of something wildly
  By us performed before. Most dearly welcome!
  And your fair princess—goddess! O, alas!
  I lost a couple that between heaven and earth
  Might thus have stood begetting wonder as
  You, gracious couple, do. And then I lost—
  All my own folly—the society,
  Amity too, of your brave father, whom,
  Though bearing misery, I desire on my life
  Once more to look on him.
FLORIZEL   By his command
  Have I here touched Sicilia, and from him
  Give you all greetings that a king, at friend,
  Can send his brother; and, but infirmity
  Which waits upon worn times has something seized
  His wished ability, he had himself
  The lands and waters between your throne and his
  Measured to look upon you, whom he loves—
  He bade me say so—more than all the sceptres
  And those that bear them living.
LEONTES   O my brother,
  Good gentleman, the wrongs I have done you stir
  Afresh within me, and these your offices,

So rarely kind, are as interpreters
Of my behindhand slackness. Welcome hither,
As is the spring to the earth. And has he too
Exposed this paragon to the fearful usage,
At least ungentle, of the dreadful Neptune,
To greet a man not worth her pains, much less
The adventure of her person?

FLORIZEL   Good my lord,
She came from Libya.

LEONTES   Where the warlike Smalus,
That noble honored lord, is feared and loved?

FLORIZEL
Most royal sir, from thence, from him, whose daughter
His tears proclaimed his, parting with her. Thence,
A prosperous south-wind friendly, we have crossed,
To execute the charge my father gave me
For visiting your highness. My best train
I have from your Sicilian shores dismissed,
Who for Bohemia bend, to signify
Not only my fortune in Libya, sir,
But my arrival and my wife's in safety
Here where we are.

LEONTES   The blessèd gods
Purge all infection from our air while you
Do climate here! You have a holy father,
A graceful gentleman, against whose person,
So sacred as it is, I have done sin,
For which the heavens, taking angry note,
Have left me issueless; and your father's blest,
As he from heaven merits it, with you,
Worthy his goodness. What might I have been,
Might I a son and daughter now have looked on,
Such goodly things as you?

Enter a Lord.

LORD   Most noble sir,
   That which I shall report will bear no credit,
   Were not the proof so nigh. Please you, great sir,
   Bohemia greets you from himself by me,
   Desires you to attach his son, who has—
   His dignity and duty both cast off—
   Fled from his father, from his hopes, and with
   A shepherd's daughter.

LEONTES   Where's Bohemia? Speak.

LORD
   Here in your city. I now came from him.
   I speak amazedly, and it becomes
   My marvel and my message. To your Court
   While he was hastening—in the chase, it seems,
   Of this fair couple—meets he on the way
   The father of this seeming lady and
   Her brother, having both their country quitted
   With this young prince.

FLORIZEL   Camillo has betrayed me,
   Whose honor and whose honesty till now
   Endured all weathers.

LORD   Lay it so to his charge.
   He is with the king your father.

LEONTES   Who? Camillo?

LORD
   Camillo, sir. I spoke with him, who now
   Has these poor men in question. Never saw I
   Wretches so quake. They kneel, they kiss the earth,
   Forswear themselves as often as they speak.
   Bohemia stops his ears, and threatens them
   With divers deaths in death.

PERDITA   O my poor father!
   The heaven sets spies upon us, will not have
   Our contract celebrated.

LEONTES   You are married?

FLORIZEL
    We are not, sir, nor are we likely to be.
    The stars, I see, will kiss the valleys first;
    The odds for high and low are alike.
LEONTES   My lord,
    Is this the daughter of a king?
FLORIZEL   She is
    When once she is my wife.
LEONTES
    That 'once,' I see by your good father's speed,
    Will come on very slowly. I am sorry,
    Most sorry, you have broken from his liking
    Where you were tied in duty, and as sorry
    Your choice is not so rich in worth as beauty,
    That you might well enjoy her.
FLORIZEL   Dear, look up.
    Though Fortune, visible an enemy,
    Should chase us with my father, power no jot
    Has she to change our loves. Beseech you, sir,
    Remember since you owed no more to time
    Than I do now. With thought of such affections,
    Step forth my advocate. At your request
    My father will grant precious things as trifles.
LEONTES
    Would he do so, I'd beg your precious mistress,
    Which he counts but a trifle.
PAULINA   Sir, my liege,
    Your eye has too much youth in it. Not a month
    Before your queen died, she was more worth such gazes
    Than what you look on now.
LEONTES   I thought of her
    Even in these looks I made. [to Florizel] But your
      petition
    Is yet unanswered. I will to your father.
    Your honor not overthrown by your desires,
    I am friend to them and you. Upon which errand

I now go toward him; therefore follow me
And mark what way I make. Come, good my lord.

Exeunt.

SCENE II
Before Leontes' palace.

Enter Autolycus and a Gentleman.

AUTOLYCUS Beseech you, sir, were you present at this
relation?

FIRST GENTLEMAN I was by at the opening of the bundle,
heard the old shepherd deliver the manner how he
found it; whereupon, after a little amazedness, we were
all commanded out of the chamber. Only this I thought
I heard the shepherd say, he found the child.

AUTOLYCUS I would most gladly know the issue of it.

FIRST GENTLEMAN I make a broken delivery of the
business; but the changes I perceived in the king and
Camillo were very notes of admiration. They seemed
almost, with staring on one another, to tear the cases of
their eyes. There was speech in their dumbness, language
in their very gesture. They looked as they had heard of a
world ransomed, or one destroyed. A notable passion of
wonder appeared in them. But the wisest beholder, that
knew no more but seeing, could not say if the importance
were joy or sorrow; but in the extremity of the one, it
must needs be.

Enter another Gentleman.

Here comes a gentleman that haply knows more. The
news, Rogero?

SECOND GENTLEMAN Nothing but bonfires. The oracle
is fulfilled; the king's daughter is found. Such a deal of

wonder is broken out within this hour that balladmakers
cannot be able to express it.

Enter another Gentleman.

Here comes the Lady Paulina's steward; he can deliver
you more. How goes it now, sir? This news which is
called true is so like an old tale that the verity of it is in
strong suspicion. Has the king found his heir?

THIRD GENTLEMAN Most true, if ever truth were pregnant
by circumstance. That which you hear you will swear
you see, there is such unity in the proofs. The mantle of
Queen Hermione's, her jewel about the neck of it, the
letters of Antigonus found with it, which they know to
be his hand; the majesty of the creature in resemblance
of the mother, the affection of nobleness which nature
shows above her breeding, and many other evidences
proclaim her with all certainty to be the king's daughter.
Did you see the meeting of the two kings?

SECOND GENTLEMAN No.

THIRD GENTLEMAN Then have you lost a sight which
was to be seen, cannot be spoken of. There might you
have beheld one joy crown another, so and in such
manner that it seemed sorrow wept to take leave of
them, for their joy waded in tears. There was casting up
of eyes, holding up of hands, with countenance of such
distraction that they were to be known by garment, not
by features. Our king, being ready to leap out of himself
for joy of his found daughter, as if that joy were now
become a loss, cries, 'O, your mother, your mother!'
then asks Bohemia forgiveness; then embraces his son-in-
law; then again worries he his daughter with enfolding
her. Now he thanks the old shepherd, who stands by
like a weather-bitten conduit of many kings' reigns. I
never heard of such another encounter, which lames
report to follow it and undoes description to do it.

SECOND GENTLEMAN What, pray you, became of
Antigonus, that carried hence the child?

THIRD GENTLEMAN Like an old tale still, which will have
matter to rehearse, though credit be asleep and not an
ear open. He was torn to pieces by a bear. This avouches
the shepherd's son, who has not only his innocence,
which seems much, to justify him, but a handkerchief
and rings of his that Paulina knows.

FIRST GENTLEMAN What became of his bark and his
followers?

THIRD GENTLEMAN Wrecked the same instant of their
master's death and in the view of the shepherd; so that
all the instruments which aided to expose the child
were even then lost when it was found. But O, the noble
combat that between joy and sorrow was fought in
Paulina! She had one eye declined for the loss of her
husband, another elevated that the oracle was fulfilled.
She lifted the princess from the earth, and so locks her
in embracing as if she would pin her to her heart that
she might no more be in danger of losing.

FIRST GENTLEMAN The dignity of this act was worth the
audience of kings and princes, for by such was it acted.

THIRD GENTLEMAN One of the prettiest touches of all,
and that which angled for my eyes, caught the water
though not the fish, was when, at the relation of the
queen's death, with the manner how she came to it
bravely confessed and lamented by the king, how
attentiveness wounded his daughter. Till, from one sign
of dolor to another, she did, with an 'Alas,' I would fain
say, bleed tears, for I am sure my heart wept blood. Who
was most marble there changed color; some swooned,
all sorrowed. If all the world could have seen it, the woe
had been universal.

FIRST GENTLEMAN Are they returned to the court?

THIRD GENTLEMAN No. The princess, hearing of her
mother's statue, which is in the keeping of Paulina—a

piece many years in doing and now newly performed by
that rare Italian master, Julio Romano; who, had he
himself eternity and could put breath into his work,
would beguile Nature of her custom, so perfectly he is
her ape. He so near to Hermione has done Hermione
that they say one would speak to her and stand in hope
of answer. Thither with all greediness of affection are
they gone, and there they intend to sup.

SECOND GENTLEMAN I thought she had some great matter
there in hand, for she has privately twice or thrice a
day, ever since the death of Hermione, visited that
removed house. Shall we thither and with our company
piece the rejoicing?

FIRST GENTLEMAN Who would be thence that has the
benefit of access? Every wink of an eye some new grace
will be born. Our absence makes us unthrifty to our
knowledge. Let's along.   *Exeunt Gentlemen.*

AUTOLYCUS Now, had I not the dash of my former life in
me would preferment drop on my head. I brought the
old man and his son aboard the prince, told him I heard
them talk of a bundle and I know not what. But he at
that time, over-fond of the shepherd's daughter—so he
then took her to be—who began to be much seasick, and
himself little better, extremity of weather continuing,
this mystery remained undiscovered. But it is all one to
me; for had I been the finder out of this secret, it would
not have relished among my other discredits.

Enter Shepherd and Clown.

Here come those I have done good to against my will,
and already appearing in the blossoms of their fortune.

SHEPHERD Come, boy. I am past more children, but your
sons and daughters will be all gentlemen born.

CLOWN You are well met, sir. You denied to fight with me
this other day, because I was no gentleman born. See

you these clothes? Say you see them not and think me
still no gentleman born! You were best say these robes
are not gentlemen born. Give me the lie, do, and try
whether I am not now a gentleman born.

AUTOLYCUS I know you are now, sir, a gentleman born.

CLOWN Ay, and have been so any time these four hours.

SHEPHERD And so have I, boy.

CLOWN So you have. But I was a gentleman born before
my father, for the king's son took me by the hand and
called me brother; and then the two kings called my
father brother; and then the prince my brother and the
princess my sister called my father father. And so we
wept, and there were the first gentleman-like tears that
ever we shed.

SHEPHERD We may live, son, to shed many more.

CLOWN Ay, or else it were hard luck, being in so
preposterous estate as we are.

AUTOLYCUS I humbly beseech you, sir, to pardon me all
the faults I have committed to your worship and to give
me your good report to the prince my master.

SHEPHERD Pray, son, do, for we must be gentle now we are
gentlemen.

CLOWN You will amend your life?

AUTOLYCUS Ay, if it likes your good worship.

CLOWN Give me your hand. I will swear to the prince you
are as honest a true fellow as any is in Bohemia.

SHEPHERD You may say it, but not swear it.

CLOWN Not swear it, now I am a gentleman? Let boors
and franklins say it, I'll swear it.

SHEPHERD How if it is false, son?

CLOWN If it is never so false, a true gentleman may swear
it in the behalf of his friend. And I'll swear to the prince
you are a tall fellow of your hands and that you will not
be drunk. But I know you are no tall fellow of your
hands and that you will be drunk. But I'll swear it, and
I would you would be a tall fellow of your hands.

AUTOLYCUS I will prove so, sir, to my power.

CLOWN Ay, by any means prove a tall fellow. If I do not
wonder how you dare venture to be drunk, not being a
tall fellow, trust me not. Hark! The kings and the
princes, our kindred, are going to see the queen's picture.
Come, follow us. We'll be your good masters.

Exeunt.

SCENE III
Paulina's house.

*Enter Leontes, Polixenes, Florizel, Perdita, Camillo,
Paulina, Lords, and Attendants.*

LEONTES
O grave and good Paulina, the great comfort
That I have had of you!

PAULINA   What, sovereign sir,
I did not well, I meant well. All my services
You have paid home. But that you have vouchsafed,
With your crowned brother and these your contracted
Heirs of your kingdoms, my poor house to visit,
It is a surplus of your grace which never
My life may last to answer.

LEONTES   O Paulina,
We honor you with trouble. But we came
To see the statue of our queen. Your gallery
Have we passed through, not without much content
In many singularities; but we saw not
That which my daughter came to look upon,
The statue of her mother.

PAULINA   As she lived peerless,
So her dead likeness, I do well believe,
Excels whatever yet you looked upon
Or hand of man has done. Therefore I keep it

Lonely, apart. But here it is. Prepare
To see the life as lively mocked as ever
Still sleep mocked death. Behold, and say it is well.

Paulina reveals Hermione standing like a statue.

I like your silence; it the more shows off
Your wonder. But yet speak; first, you, my liege.
Comes it not something near?
LEONTES   Her natural posture!
Chide me, dear stone, that I may say indeed
You are Hermione; or rather, you are she
In your not chiding, for she was as tender
As infancy and grace. But yet, Paulina,
Hermione was not so much wrinkled, nothing
So aged as this seems.
POLIXENES   O, not by much.
PAULINA
So much the more our carver's excellence,
Which lets go by some sixteen years and makes her
As if she lived now.
LEONTES   As now she might have done,
So much to my good comfort, as it is
Now piercing to my soul. O, thus she stood,
Even with such life of majesty—warm life,
As now it coldly stands—when first I wooed her!
I am ashamed. Does not the stone rebuke me
For being more stone than it? O royal piece,
There's magic in your majesty, which has
My evils conjured to remembrance and
From your admiring daughter took the spirit,
Standing like stone with you.
PERDITA   And give me leave,
And do not say it is superstition, that
I kneel and then implore her blessing. Lady,

Dear queen, that ended when I but began,
Give me that hand of yours to kiss.
PAULINA   O, patience!
The statue is but newly fixed, the color's
Not dry.
CAMILLO
My lord, your sorrow was too sore laid on,
Which sixteen winters cannot blow away,
So many summers dry. Scarce any joy
Did ever so long live; no sorrow
But killed itself much sooner.
POLIXENES   Dear my brother,
Let him that was the cause of this have power
To take off so much grief from you as he
Will piece up in himself.
PAULINA   Indeed, my lord,
If I had thought the sight of my poor image
Would thus have wrought you—for the stone is mine—
I'd not have shown it.
LEONTES   Do not draw the curtain.
PAULINA
No longer shall you gaze on it, lest your fancy
May think anon it moves.
LEONTES   Let be, let be.
Would I were dead, but that, I think, already—
What was he that did make it? See, my lord,
Would you not deem it breathed? and that those veins
Did verily bear blood?
POLIXENES   Masterly done.
The very life seems warm upon her lip.
LEONTES
The fixture of her eye has motion in it,
As we are mocked with art.
PAULINA   I'll draw the curtain.
My lord is almost so far transported that
He will think anon it lives.

LEONTES   O sweet Paulina,
  Make me to think so twenty years together!
  No settled senses of the world can match
  The pleasure of that madness. Let it alone.
PAULINA
  I am sorry, sir, I have thus far stirred you; but
  I could afflict you farther.
LEONTES   Do, Paulina,
  For this affliction has a taste as sweet
  As any cordial comfort. Still it seems
  There is an air comes from her. What fine chisel
  Could ever yet cut breath? Let no man mock me,
  For I will kiss her.
PAULINA   Good my lord, forbear.
  The ruddiness upon her lip is wet;
  You'll mar it if you kiss it, stain your own
  With oily painting. Shall I draw the curtain?
LEONTES
  No, not these twenty years.
PERDITA   So long could I
  Stand by, a looker on.
PAULINA   Either forbear,
  Quit presently the chapel, or resolve you
  For more amazement. If you can behold it,
  I'll make the statue move indeed, descend
  And take you by the hand. But then you'll think—
  Which I protest against—I am assisted
  By wicked powers.
LEONTES   What you can make her do,
  I am content to look on; what to speak,
  I am content to hear, for it is as easy
  To make her speak as move.
PAULINA   It is required
  You do awake your faith. Then all stand still;
  Or those that think it is unlawful business
  I am about, let them depart.

LEONTES   Proceed.
  No foot shall stir.
PAULINA   Music! Awake her, strike!

[Music.]

  It is time; descend; be stone no more; approach;
  Strike all that look upon with marvel. Come,
  I'll fill your grave up. Stir, nay, come away;
  Bequeath to death your numbness, for from him
  Dear life redeems you. You perceive she stirs.

Hermione comes down.

  Start not; her actions shall be holy as
  You hear my spell is lawful. Do not shun her
  Until you see her die again, for then
  You kill her doubly. Nay, present your hand.
  When she was young you wooed her; now in age
  Is she become the suitor?
LEONTES   O, she is warm!
  If this is magic, let it be an art
  Lawful as eating.
POLIXENES   She embraces him.
CAMILLO
  She hangs about his neck.
  If she pertains to life, let her speak too.
POLIXENES
  Ay, and make it manifest where she has lived,
  Or how stolen from the dead.
PAULINA   That she is living,
  Were it but told you should be hooted at
  Like an old tale; but it appears she lives,
  Though yet she speaks not. Mark a little while.
  Please you to interpose, fair madam. Kneel

And pray your mother's blessing. Turn, good lady;
Our Perdita is found.

HERMIONE   You gods, look down,
And from your sacred vials pour your graces
Upon my daughter's head! Tell me, my own,
Where have you been preserved? where lived? how found
Your father's Court? For you shall hear that I,
Knowing by Paulina that the oracle
Gave hope you were in being, have preserved
Myself to see the issue.

PAULINA   There's time enough for that,
Lest they desire upon this push to trouble
Your joys with like relation. Go together,
You precious winners all; your exultation
Partake to every one. I, an old turtle-dove
Will wing me to some withered bough and there
My mate, that's never to be found again,
Lament till I am lost.

LEONTES   O, peace, Paulina!
You should a husband take by my consent,
As I by yours a wife. This is a match,
And made between us by vows. You have found mine;
But how, is to be questioned, for I saw her,
As I thought, dead, and have in vain said many
A prayer upon her grave. I'll not seek far—
For him, I partly know his mind—to find you
An honorable husband. Come, Camillo,
And take her by the hand, whose worth and honesty
Are richly noted and here justified
By us, a pair of kings. Let's from this place.
What! look upon my brother. Both your pardons,
That ever I put between your holy looks
My ill suspicion. This your son-in-law
And son unto the king, whom heavens directing,
Is troth-plight to your daughter. Good Paulina,
Lead us from hence, where we may leisurely

Each one demand and answer to his part
Performed in this wide gap of time, since first
We were dissevered. Hastily lead away.   *Exeunt.*